BLOCKHEAD

BLOCKHEAD

VENTURING INTO THE BRAVE NEW WORLD
OF BITCOIN, BLOCKCHAIN TECHNOLOGY,
AND CRYPTOCURRENCY TRADING

KAIN OSTERHOLT

COPYRIGHT © 2024 KAIN OSTERHOLT
All rights reserved.

BLOCKHEAD
Venturing into the Brave New World of Bitcoin, Blockchain Technology, and Cryptocurrency Trading

FIRST EDITION

ISBN   978-1-5445-4515-8   *Hardcover*
       978-1-5445-4514-1   *Paperback*
       978-1-5445-4513-4   *Ebook*

To Dad, for teaching me how to be curious and learn new things.

CONTENTS

INTRODUCTION 9

PART I: BIRTH OF THE DIGITAL AGE AND BITCOIN
1. NEW PARADIGM 19
2. BITCOIN MECHANICS 39
3. LIFE BEFORE BITCOIN 51

PART II: THE BITCOIN CYCLES
4. CYCLE 1 67
5. CYCLE 2 77
6. CYCLE 3 91
7. CYCLE 4 119

PART III: LEARNING FROM THE PAST, SPECULATING ON THE FUTURE
8. LESSONS LEARNED 149
9. THE FUTURE 163
10. THE BIG PIVOT 175

GLOSSARY 187

INTRODUCTION

Relative to the time human beings have been investing their surplus capital in markets, Bitcoin and other cryptocurrencies represent only a small sliver of recent history, and yet it feels like a lifetime ago that these digital assets first took hold of my interest. In 2011, roughly six years after I graduated from college, my dad pointed me to an article describing a new type of "currency" that would eventually become a controversial spectacle on the world stage. Before Bitcoin was a well-known term in the investment community's lexicon, a small online group formed to discuss the possibilities of a future where a form of money native to the internet would change the world for the better.

 YouTube, a video-streaming platform known for non-mainstream content and relatively new at the time, would prove to be a deep rabbit hole full of Bitcoin speculation, philosophy, education, and entertainment. Some early adopters were already making videos, discussing the philosophy of storing value, **fractional-reserve banking**, and **fiat money**. The US economy had recently collapsed in 2008, just three years before I discovered this burgeoning movement, and to an impressionable young engineer, Bitcoin appeared to be the solution for everything wrong with money. The hidden forces of nature that we call emotions took hold, and I couldn't sit still with only fiat currency knowing the illegitimacy that existed in the monetary system.

In the summer of 2011, I purchased my first "bag" of Bitcoin at around $15 each on **Mt. Gox**, and the roller-coaster ride that ensued became far beyond any experience I could have imagined. This book is an attempt to present my experiences owning and trading Bitcoin (and other cryptocurrencies) throughout the period between late 2011 and 2022 in hopes that my retrospective analysis and deep dive into the decision-making process bring value to all who are interested in the space, including newcomers and experienced veterans.

The book is split into three parts: (1) Birth of the Digital Age and Bitcoin, (2) The Bitcoin Cycles, and (3) Learning from the Past, Speculating on the Future. The reader is provided with a glossary of terms to add extra detail to the understanding of a concept, but the content does not cater to a beginner starting with a blank slate. A reader with some basic knowledge and experience in **cryptocurrency** trading will get the most out of this book.

The history of money, capital markets, and how it ties into the digital age is the subject of Chapter 1. In this primer, I'll discuss what led us to this era of social media and Bitcoin so that readers will get a good understanding of the thesis behind internet money. Any good investment starts with research, and the digital asset space continues to evolve year after year, along with digital technologies at large. Some key concepts will underscore the mechanisms that drive Bitcoin's value, which can be derived from the properties of money that have held true through millennia as various forms of money have been both created and left behind. Although some might say Bitcoin doesn't have any intrinsic value, I'll challenge those arguments by first providing a history that ties the inception of modern money and the digital age together. Understanding the long trajectory leading up to the creation of Bitcoin and **blockchain** technology, in general, can provide insight into where things are headed in the future.

In Chapter 2, I'll discuss the mechanics of Bitcoin and how to acquire/store the asset. This chapter is primarily for readers who missed the early days when Bitcoin first launched. An experienced Bitcoiner may want to skip Chapter 2, but it can be useful to get another perspective on the fundamentals.

In Chapter 3, I tell my life story as it leads up to my discovery of Bitcoin in 2011. By providing a background on how I grew up and dealt with finances, I believe readers will gain an understanding of me and my generation. Why is it that I was drawn into cryptocurrencies? Why spend a lot of time and effort learning about how money and markets work?

Throughout my time in the digital assets space, I have come to notice the intricate evolutionary process of the overall market mindset. I elucidate further how the long-term trajectory might inform us of what we can expect in the future. This requires not only an analysis of the price of an asset but also the emotions and reasoning behind a trade or investment. For some, this may be considered too subjective or illogical. Surely, this must be a game of mathematics, chart analysis, and scientific reasoning about economics, right? Even the experts, the scientists, the economists, and the world's best algo-trading bots get things wrong, and this is proof that there is something more to the story. An investor who has experienced a **market cycle** will most likely be familiar with the following chart:

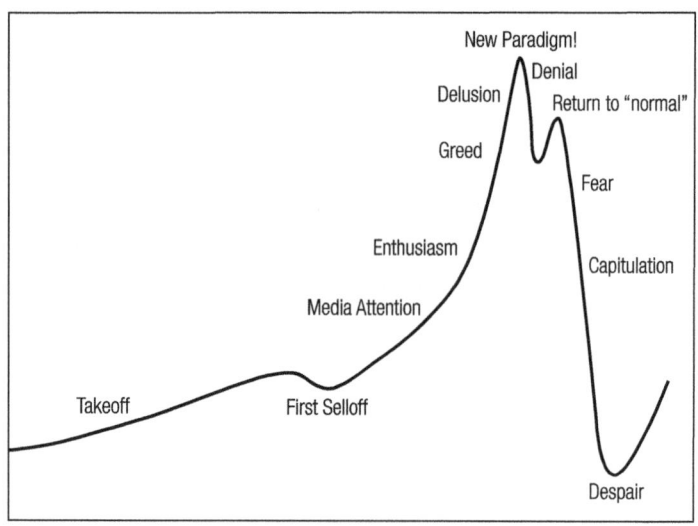

Figure 1

Chapters 4 through 7 tell the story of each Bitcoin bubble cycle, each with its own unique fingerprint representing market growth, technological advancement, and reactions to events in shorter-term time frames, which leads price action to follow characteristics that fit the classic bubble pattern familiar to experienced traders. In Figure 1 depicting the phases of a bubble, it may be interesting to those unfamiliar with this classic pattern that emotions, not only monetary or network-value characteristics, are used to describe the stages. For example, greed comes just before delusion in the chart. These terms are not strictly scientific-economic events or math equations. They are feelings that individuals and the crowd at large experience as the stages progress. These subjective temperaments are just as important as the technical analysis for an inexperienced trader to understand, so I will discuss them in detail in Chapter 4 as I describe the market cycles from a first-person perspective. Figure 2 is a Bitcoin price chart annotated to point out when I made my first Bitcoin purchase.

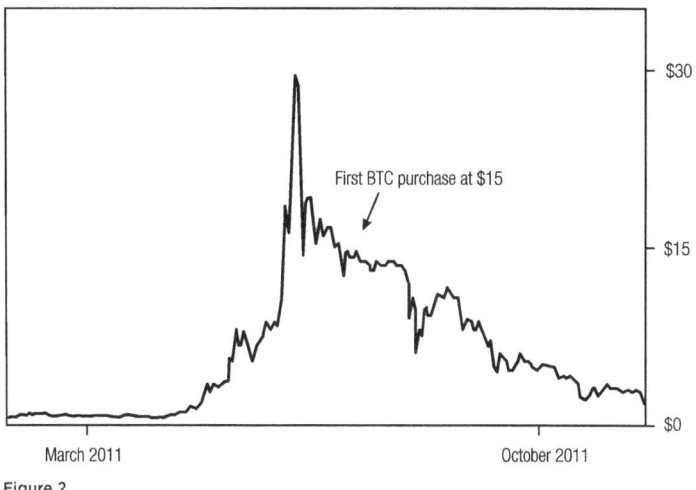

Figure 2

When the price of Bitcoin reached $30 and lost nearly half its value at $15, I thought I was getting a fantastic deal! I had done my research, and this was a once-in-a-lifetime invention that was going to change the world of money. So what happened? Why did Bitcoin over the next four months decline to about $2? Can you imagine how I felt in those days, watching so much value melt away? In Chapter 4, I will go over this in detail when I describe Cycle 1, but for introductory purposes, this helps paint the picture of what it might feel like to know despair in the most visceral way. This represents hard-earned money that I had saved in my six years as a professional, still working my way out of student loan debt, an auto loan, and a mortgage. Emotional memory of those losses would later come in handy, but as I mentioned before, the market evolves, presenting new opportunities and behaviors that don't exactly match previous trends. The market evolving coupled with making subsequent decisions based on previous lessons means that the process of investing is a never-ending feedback loop of experiences and lessons that can be utilized in the future. These lessons, along with reflecting on historical data and analysis to assist in developing new strategies, then provide more unique outcomes to process.

One of the reasons I am writing this book is to show through experience that prior historical data does not predict future outcomes. There are many popular sources of analysis and trading tips that are based on historical trends, which imply some pattern that will play out again in the future, and any number of information sources attempting to hype up a new and/or unproven project by enticing new money to jump in and invest. My time in this market has resulted in both short-term lessons and a longer-term understanding of which strategies I'm more comfortable with. I will go into detail on these lessons in Chapter 8.

In Chapter 9, I delve into some concepts that are likely to influence the future of Bitcoin and the digital age. Bitcoin's colorful past is only the beginning of something that continues to evolve and develop into what might be a very commonly used tool.

Finally, in Chapter 10, I conclude with some cautionary thoughts about the way that central banks currently manage monetary policy and how it is affecting markets. A fight against inflation comes with certain costs to the economy, and the lengthy period where easy money seemed to be never ending is directly related to asset bubbles, which could end up deflating. But will this uncertain period lead to the death of Bitcoin?

As I write this on Saturday, June 18, 2022, Bitcoin is trading at almost $19,000 after reaching an all-time high of roughly $69,000 only seven months earlier. During a downturn like this, there are typically media outlets and pundits who like to claim that Bitcoin is dead, and thus there is a website dedicated to Bitcoin obituaries (https://99bitcoins.com/bitcoin-obituaries/). However, there are **memes** designed to disprove these naysayers' banal announcements. Looking at the long-term chart, including all of Bitcoin's price history, it is apparent that something interesting is repeating over a longer-term time frame.

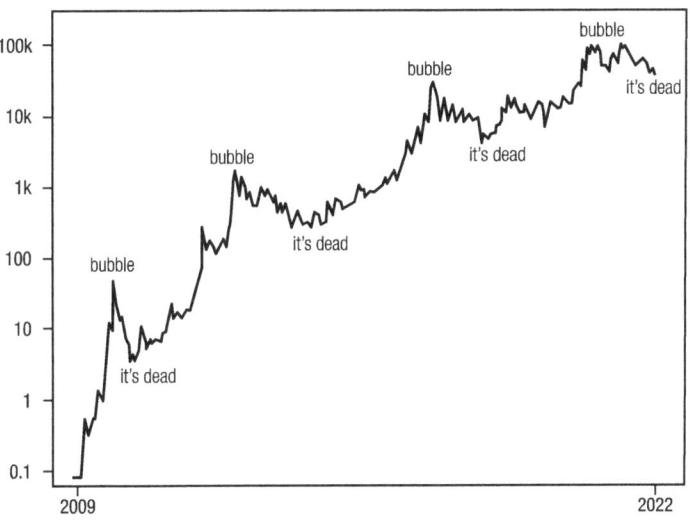

Figure 3

As shown in Figure 3, every time the Bitcoin price rises to "bubble" levels, it reverts to a **logarithmic regression** pattern that can be seen by ignoring the short-term noise. This pattern is like the curve that represents the number of people who adopted the internet in the '90s and into the 2000s. There are very few people who invested in Bitcoin in its early days of existence and even fewer people in that cohort who had the fortitude to simply hold on to the investment through the ups and downs. With the rise in popularity of digital technology and waves of innovation replacing legacy systems, I suspect that the roller-coaster ride we call the world economy will continue to challenge new participants and seasoned veterans as the landscape of investing continues to change. The story that follows is an attempt to capture a small but important piece of that evolutionary process.

PART I

BIRTH OF THE DIGITAL AGE AND BITCOIN

CHAPTER 1

NEW PARADIGM

Long before there was a need for modern money, our early human ancestors survived in what may have been early forms of communes as on-demand hunter-gatherers. Basic needs were met in a small community of residents who all participated in the day-to-day work required to survive and keep life moving forward with each new generation. Not much was wasted, but not much was saved either because, without modern tools to store food and other resources, there were no incentives to amass wealth and store it for long periods of time if the community was happy and well fed each day. However, life was much more fragile in those times, and when food, water, or other essentials for sustaining life were scarce for various reasons, such as a climate disaster or any other unexpected derailment, it could often pose an existential risk. In some cases, it could lead to the extinction of entire family lines. This set of life conditions motivated people to solve such a problem by inventing ways of creating an abundance of food and storing it for emergencies.

Eventually, agricultural entrepreneurship took shape to solve the problems of the volatile feast-and-famine cycle.

The solution to the problem of starvation due to the uncertain nature of on-demand food acquisition via hunting and/or gathering was long-term storage of reserves and scaling up production. Food reserves were stores of wealth that could be traded on a market, but this process of migration and enhancing tools that could be leveraged to produce necessities for life took hundreds of thousands of years. Historical evidence suggests that by 8000 BCE, people started to form larger-scale agriculture operations in ancient Sumeria, or lands that are part of Iraq today. This eventually led to the emergence of complex networks connecting cities and more complex markets that required yet more innovations to solve new problems as societies evolved.

The ability to amass a surplus creates yet another issue: how should a farmer store and/or distribute this newfound form of wealth, and how can it be exchanged if a buyer doesn't have what the farmer wants? This dilemma is known as the *coincidence of wants* problem. If Bob has bananas and Jane has apples, they can trade if each person wants what the other has to offer. However, even assuming this is the case, it may still be difficult to determine how much of one item can be traded for the other. This issue would be solved if there were some items that everyone agrees stores a certain amount of value that can be exchanged for goods and/or services. This is why money was introduced to maximize efficiency in markets where surplus goods and services can be bought and sold.

Forms of money emerged throughout history in isolated environments, indicating that evolving societies create money out of necessity because of the way its properties tend to increase efficiency in markets and therefore lead to a more prosperous existence for market participants. Widely accepted forms of money tend to have some or all of the following attributes:

- **Fungible**—A unit of money is not discernible from any other unit of money in the existing supply. This isn't always as simple as it sounds since serial numbers or markings and patterns on variations of currency can change the perception of value in the currency unit. For an ideal money supply, all individual units of the money are treated equally.
- **Durable**—Physical forms of money need to maintain their form to retain value in the long term. Digital forms of money need to be maintained in accounting systems but are less prone to degradation in the physical sense.
- **Portable**—Money is designed so that it can be easily taken with a person on a trip to the store to reduce friction in an economy. Physical money is usually small and light so a person can be mobile with as much as they desire to have. Digital money can typically be accessed anywhere there is a network connection that can facilitate digital communication and exchange between the participants.
- **Recognizable**—Money can be authenticated easily while also reducing the ease of creating counterfeit versions.
- **Stable**—Along with durability, the money supply should remain fixed so that it cannot be easily debased. The scarcity of an asset is the key to storing its value over time, which maintains the trust of its users and therefore preserves a trustful society.

The evolution of more complex economic activity throughout the ages motivated people to develop forms of money that improved on these traits and in some cases would require trade-offs. For example, gold isn't as portable as a piece of paper that says it is worth one hundred ounces of gold, but paper is neither as durable nor as stable as gold since it can be easily destroyed or created cheaply, which makes it susceptible to corruption. As borrowing and lending also evolved in more recent economies, even more instruments and systems were developed to provide people with more and more options to invest their surplus capital, and this led to the transition into what we now call **capitalism**.

Capitalism allows an individual or entity (such as a corporation) to invest surplus capital, trading off risk for the possibility of earning future returns on the investment. The contemporary form of capitalism experienced today in the United States and many other countries throughout the world took shape in 1602 when the Dutch East India Company became the first publicly traded entity in Amsterdam. This marked the first time owning a share of a company was made possible in a publicly traded market. This does not mean investing surplus capital and trading off risk for future returns was a new invention. However, these more complex enterprises would have been far messier and more chaotic before the advent of the public stock market. Without trustworthy governing bodies and regulators to enforce fair play in such a system, it would be easy for corrupt actors to take advantage of the weaknesses in the system, and its people.

This governance and regulatory framework, along with the ability to enforce it, are what I consider to be the **world order**. Before world-dominating empires with strong militaries and codes of law existed, much of the game theoretic motivations for pursuing wealth would have been defined by physical strength to take over other civilizations to plunder their fortunes.

Coercion and making gains using raw power, or allegiance to a higher power as in the case in theocracies, are still prevalent in various parts of the world. However, in modernized countries, these earlier forms of social governance are often frowned upon and criticized in favor of equal treatment under the Universal Declaration of Human Rights, which has been accepted by the United Nations since 1948 as the principal framework for maintaining equality under the law.

In 1602, when the stock market was first initiated in Amsterdam, the world was still a largely unexplored and unforgiving place in terms of the cultural clashes that were occurring because of exploration and imperialistic modes of engagement. Many different value systems, governments, and philosophies were colliding with each other in a process that merged cultures and synthesized new ways of thinking. This chaotic process of discovery, convergence, and synthesis over the next three to four centuries produced new sets of problems that needed solutions to maintain a relatively peaceful and fair system that allowed societies to flourish globally. This process eventually birthed the philosophy of **liberalism**.

In a liberal society with free markets, it is a goal to limit physical strength or theocratic rule as the primary driver for the accumulation of wealth so that individuals all have equality of opportunity and protections under the law in which accumulated wealth can be safely stored and invested, i.e., property rights and individual liberty. This doesn't mean that physical strength has no value in an economy, however the world order, if defined by liberal values, ideally maximizes equality under the law and provides everyone with equal opportunity regardless of physical attributes. In other words, not survival of the fittest and gains by force or prescribed roles based on religious servitude but rather preferences for incentives based on delivery of value to society and a desire to educate and develop members of society so that everyone has a chance to succeed in providing value in the system.

Liberalism was a philosophy that emerged as an evolutionary response to imperialistic and autocratic motives that arose in the Middle Ages and led to the age of Enlightenment, which ushered in scientific and technological progress defining the era of **modernity**. Throughout modernity, Western nations explored the rest of the world and implemented economies of scale in the Industrial Revolution to economize more of the existing resources while evolving politics and governments with the new framework of liberalism in mind. The United States formed under a new constitution utilizing these values and in 1789, after the American Revolution, invented one of the most modern forms of government that exists today, which allowed a powerful wave of innovation during the nineteenth and twentieth centuries to accelerate technological and intellectual progress.

Although this short version of history makes it sound like a simple process, the United States currently exists in a time of consternation over the current geopolitical situation in 2023, and many events in its history are still controversial. It took centuries for Americans, generation after generation, to understand, accept, internalize, and actualize liberal values, and it is apparent that there is still a lot of room left to progress within this value system to solve problems in our current way of life and governance. This transformation in the United States and many other Western nations is what set the stage for significant levels of prosperity throughout the world, and it remains one of the binding forces for our current world order to operate successfully as well as relatively peacefully.

The current world order is nowhere near perfect, and society's evolutionary forces guide people to challenge the status quo to develop improvements to our philosophy, politics, economics, and way of life. As people around the globe progressed and leveraged scientific breakthroughs that were produced in modernity, a new set of problems arose as the living conditions that were normalized throughout the 1800s and 1900s began to infringe on the limited resources of the planet. This growing awareness of the impossibility of achieving infinite growth by way of objective progress and the heightened awareness of the exploitation of foreign and domestic labor forces to propagate the economic machine of the world order along with capitalism's relentless focus on monetary profits without regard to ecological health led to the emergence of a new movement and new philosophical frameworks.

Modernity, through its support of scientific progress, gave humanity the tools that exposed the limitations of our existence on earth for the first time, and the awareness of this new insight led people to begin questioning modernity's assumptions, producing a new philosophy called postmodernism, gaining traction at about the same time as the transition into the digital age. Postmodernism attempts to challenge the philosophy of universal truths by proclaiming that truth is only a concept that each sentient entity learns by a process of social construction.

The truth of the individual is their truth, and society attempts to manage the truth in the minds of the people using social construction, which must be deconstructed to understand the epistemological origins of the so-called facts. In a period where information technology grew to mainstream adoption levels, it is data mining, subject targeting, and information flow that became valued significantly in a postmodern society. This data processing and targeting of individuals is what can cause each consumer of digital information to gather various versions of the truth. The widely accepted societal truths could now be challenged and the status quo disrupted once again. Understanding the progression toward the postmodern transition requires a deep dive into the history of digital information technology. New communication tools facilitated by the internet prompted a transition to rapid and near-instant engagement on a worldwide scale, and this new mode of engagement is what has allowed individuals to create their own channels of truth for the rest of the world to consume.

THE DIGITAL AGE

After the end of World War II, the **Bretton Woods Agreement** in 1944 redefined the world order, ushering in a new global monetary system with the US dollar being the world reserve currency. Only a few years later in 1947, Bell Labs scientists led by William Shockley in New Jersey developed the first operational transistor, which set the stage for an enormously impactful wave of digital innovation. Before the transistor existed, computers required large, fragile, expensive, and inefficient vacuum tubes to represent digital logic gates capable of digital computation. For example, in 1945, Electronic Numerical Integrator and Computer (ENIAC) was the first programmable digital computer. It cost $487,000 (equivalent to $5,900,000 in 2020) and weighed more than 27 tons, was roughly 8 ft × 3 ft × 100 ft (2 m × 1 m × 30 m) in size, occupied 1,800 sq ft (170 m^2) and consumed 150 kW of electricity. With the invention and proliferation of the modern transistor and other semiconductor products, computers evolved at a breakneck pace.

In 1965, Gordon Moore, one of Shockley's fellow Bell Labs scientists, predicted that the number of transistors that fit within the same space would double every one to two years and that this would continue for at least ten years. This prediction held to be accurate and is now known as **Moore's law**. Due to the exponential nature of additional computational power at less cost, space, and power consumption, it would take only a few more decades for the personal computer industry to take off and produce affordable, lightweight, efficient, and computationally powerful machines.

In 1966, complementing Moore's law and the leading breakthroughs in digital computing technology, ARPANET began work on the original internet protocols that are still used today. In 1977, ARPANET implemented the first use of **TCP/IP**, a standard for data transmission, and shortly thereafter the modern internet was born, starting out with only a handful of nodes that could interact with each other over telephone communication lines. The word "internet" refers to a network of networks, where new network nodes can be introduced to expand the system. The addition of new nodes on the network self-reinforces the utility of the whole.

The model for representing value in communications networks was developed by the co-inventor of Ethernet, Robert Metcalf, who had the insight that a network increases in value proportionally to the square of its number of total nodes. In other words, the value grows parabolically, not linearly, with the number of new participants in the system. This relationship can be easier to understand using a simple example such as a cell phone network. When the network has one cell phone user, there is no value to the user who cannot communicate with anyone using their phone. It is only when at least two users are on the network that it obtains a non-zero utility value. However, with each new user, the network grows proportionally to the square of the number of total users because, with each additional participant, all preexisting participants gain a new connection. This new number of connections represents the additional network utility to its users and therefore the value each participant gets from being a part of it. This concept of value growing geometrically with the number of users is critical to understanding how to assess the value of the internet and the growth in the value of the Bitcoin network as it gains new adopters.

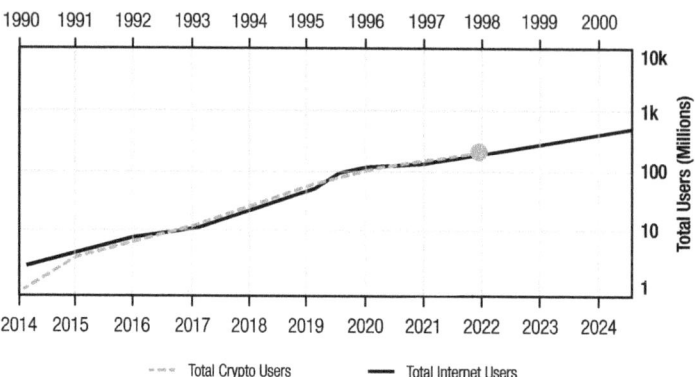

Figure 4

As an early millennial born in 1982, I was able to participate in the early growth of the internet well before my adult years. My first experiences with the internet at home were in the early 1990s, and our family seemed to be somewhat ahead of the curve when it came to using the technology. Tim Berners-Lee invented the World Wide Web in 1989 and in 1991 opened it to the public. Shortly afterward in 1994, I remember learning how to create web pages using Hypertext Markup Language (HTML). This wasn't my first experience coding since I had written some **BASIC** applications on an old TRS-80 before that. However, this was my first opportunity to develop and deliver a software creation to a network of mostly strangers on the quickly growing online information system. It wasn't immediately obvious how incredible this capability was at the time, and even then, there were not nearly as many participants in the system as there are today and far fewer websites to discover.

Imagine using the internet at a time when Google didn't exist yet, and it was still uncertain if mainstream adoption would take hold. This was a very experimental phase for the technology, and the dot-com industry was gaining traction with early adopters. It was also immature and frothy with eccentric founders and investors all competing for dominance in any web application idea conceived. Now, in 2023, the internet has subsumed a multitude of use cases, many of which were previously time consuming and tedious but now take mere seconds and minimal effort.

Consider the time and energy required to purchase a book online at Amazon.com. Using the "Buy Now" button, with a stored shipping address and payment information, it literally takes a few seconds to purchase a new book. Prior to the internet, this would have been a much more arduous process, even if the exact book was known ahead of time. Amazon also provides various options for used vs. new copies in various conditions at varying prices. This optionality is not something I remember being offered at local bookstores, when they existed in greater numbers.

I remember watching brick-and-mortar bookstores shutting down in the late nineties because of Amazon's newly discovered online shopping experience. It was a shock to the system that took down an entire physical retail category, and it seemed to happen in an instant. This example of how a simple online shopping use case had the power to dismantle a long-standing popular business model exemplifies the power of the internet. With the popularization of making online purchases instead of having to physically relocate to a store, find a product, and wait in line to make the purchase, the internet showed that it was a foundation on which new technologies could make traditional modes of existence undesirable and obsolete with relatively simple technological solutions. This pattern of internet technology taking over traditional and less-efficient processes is what led to the flood of dot-com **initial public offerings** (IPOs) in the late 1990s.

Skepticism surrounding the internet going mainstream was partly due to issues of trust, and nothing seems to require more trust than a situation that involves money and payments. If the internet could not support a trusted method of storing, sending, and receiving money, then a large share of its potential value would be untapped since the flow of money is the key to what unlocks economic activity online.

Yet another invention was necessary to make the world online safe for commerce, and that was modern encryption. Encryption alone isn't necessarily new, however; the transition to all things digital meant new problems arose in the field of security and obfuscation of information. The field of cryptography has a vast history of uses, such as the first use of ciphers in ancient Greece over two millennia ago. Fast forward to today and there are a handful of popular security techniques used in internet communications, such as Secure Sockets Layer (SSL), which can scramble data before it is sent to an end point. The end point will then know how to unscramble the data with a secure key, ensuring that the server and client are legitimate, with no bad actors in between.

When a website is secured and has a known registered certificate, a web browser typically displays the status as a lock icon somewhere in the user interface. If the connection is not secured, a modern browser will typically warn the user that they are entering a nonsecure site. With the ability to use encrypted, secure connections, internet shopping and banking were delivered to the masses online. The massive lines at bank drive-through teller systems dwindled in a similar way that bookstores became barren wastelands of useless physical space. SHA-2 encryption techniques developed at the National Security Agency (NSA) would later become a key component in securing assets on blockchains, such as Bitcoin. This will be discussed in more detail in Chapter 2: Bitcoin Mechanics.

The complete story of mainstream transformation into the digital age would not be complete without discussing mobile devices with internet connectivity. In the mid-1990s, internet-enabled laptops were mobile but only to the extent that made it possible to plug into an internet connection upon arriving at a place that had connectivity, such as an internet café. Even the introduction of wireless connections and Wi-Fi-enabled devices did not quite provide a seamless experience on the go. Wi-Fi was only available in some public areas and establishments, and the devices that had Wi-Fi capability were still inconvenient to use because of low battery life and a yet-to-be-achieved shrinking down of computer form factors that began to take shape in the late 1990s.

Mobile phones at the time were limited in capability, sometimes only providing the ability to just make calls. This would change dramatically when mobile phones and personal data assistants (PDAs) developed new internet capabilities on the go. One of the most popular companies at the time was Palm, which launched version 1.0 of Palm OS in 1996 on the Palm Pilot 1000, which did not have internet capabilities. It wasn't until 1999 that the Palm Pilot VII with 1MB of RAM and a 160 x 160 pixel monochrome display could reach some websites through its Palm.net service. Most pocket-sized mobile devices made use of a stylus (a pencil-shaped tool) that would frequently get lost or damaged, causing many headaches for customers. Sometimes it doesn't pay to be first, and Palm failed to satisfy its user-base demand for Microsoft Outlook access, and RIM was able to better capture the market with its BlackBerry lineup of devices.

Motorola also delivered some noteworthy products at the time, but there was another player on the playground with a modest $100 billion market cap that had a pocket-sized device called the iPod. Apple would eventually shake up the world with a new version of the pocket-sized device that not only had music capabilities but also phone and internet capabilities with a screen that supported multi-touch and wide-video formats. Apple launched the iPhone in 2007, and within a few years, Android-based phones became popular because they copied the multi-touch interface in a similar way that Microsoft lifted the desktop from Apple in the early 1980s with its first Windows PCs.

Within a few iterations of the iPhone and popular Android devices, the internet was officially mobile. I remember buying the first iPhone at an AT&T store in Peoria, Illinois, and moving back to Chicago with the power of Google Maps in my pocket. I couldn't believe the utility value of being able to navigate my way through the city in real time. Within a few years, every app imaginable seemed to appear on the App Store, expanding the capabilities of the device class, which quickly made mobile phones a must-have item.

The proliferation of mobile phones today and how often they are used is unprecedented. According to Pew Research Center, in May 2011, only 35 percent of Americans owned a smartphone, and in February 2021, that percentage had increased to 85 percent. Reviews.org data shows that Americans use their smartphone for an average of two hours and fifty-four minutes each day, which comes out to roughly 1.5 months of usage every year.

What often seems forgotten about society's foray into the digital age is that the internet and other computer technology started out as an obscure and unfashionable endeavor, and it wasn't necessarily welcomed by the mainstream right away; in fact, it was quite the opposite. A proclivity for technology in those days was often met with bullying. The word "nerd" was still exclusively used in a derogatory way, often used to insult anyone for talking about science, computers, the internet, video games, and other techie subjects. Now it seems that being nerdy is desirable. I've seen online dating profiles of women who desire a nerdy partner, but in 1995, it was not cool to be conscious of the impending computer revolution, nor would it have been popular to predict that people would end up being obsessed with their phones and social media.

Traditional entrepreneurs who had invested heavily in existing product solutions that were easily replaced by the internet also had an incentive to deter people from adopting the new technology trends. The naysayers were either wrong or defeated time and time again as the internet and new devices that gained capabilities such as tether-free participation quickly became the norm. This theme of resistance to adopting new technologies is nothing new, and it also applies to new forms of money and the adoption processes that take place as trust in new systems reaches critical levels of mass adoption.

PHASES OF MONEY

In *Simulacra and Simulation*, Jean Baudrillard explains that there are successive phases by which a sign is a simulacrum and eventually becomes a simulation:

1. It is the reflection of a profound reality.
2. It masks and denatures a profound reality.
3. It masks the absence of a profound reality.
4. It has no relation to any reality whatsoever: it is its own pure simulacrum.

Although Baudrillard presents these phases in the context of symbols and artifacts of our culture at the time of publication in 1981, the four phases are applicable to many other concepts including money. If money is a store of excess capital, then it is the reflection of someone's efforts to produce goods and/or services, a reflection of a profound reality in Phase 1. Money in this sense is as close to reality as possible, and to achieve this status, money itself requires work to create. Gold, for example, is mined at a cost of human labor and resources that prevent the monetary value of the element from becoming rapidly debased when compared to other physical elements that have similar properties of money. This scarcity component of precious metals determines a large portion of their monetary value, and gold is still held in central bank vaults today because it represents the excess capital exchanged by civilizations throughout history and reflects this profound reality of the existing world order. But money didn't stop here in this scarce representational form. Throughout history, empires have risen and fallen, and most if not all of them seem to have carried out an eerily predictable universal sequence.

In Phase 2, banks emerge to deliver borrowing and lending services. After all, money is not doing much just sitting there under the saver's mattress. A bank can typically lend more liability than the capital that is stored in a savings account via fractional-reserve lending. It is in this way that banks create new money on paper in hopes that the borrower can pay back the loan, including interest, which is yet more nonexistent money. This is why a traditional savings account pays interest to the saver. Every time a loan is issued, it denatures all money in the system by requiring that somehow, more of it come into existence in the future and adds to the total supply of money in the system. Under the gold standard in the United States, before there was a Federal Reserve Bank established in 1913, banks were smaller and more decentralized institutions that would settle transactions in gold. However, because the denatured money supply eventually grows to outweigh the solvency of the system, the paper money eventually masks the absence of the actual gold that exists to back it up, and it is at this point that the system tends to move into Phase 3.

In Phase 3, serious pain and corruption can occur because it is at this point when governmental powers have milked the system for more than it's worth, and a run on the banks can cause a chaotic death spiral due to insolvency risk, furthering depositors' motivations to withdraw their savings. Even the legitimate actors in the system are punished for the feckless behavior of others who led the mass corruption. At a certain point, the system requires a final intervention that sends the system into Phase 4, a monetary supply with value based solely on belief, with no gold, goods, or work to back it up. Phase 4 is the phase of fiat, meaning by decree or pure simulation of value.

At its outset under a new constitution, the United States created its mint in Philadelphia in 1792, producing coins made with silver and eventually adding gold coins in 1795. Many variations of paper money also existed, and many of these were interest-bearing bonds issued by banks, while treasury-issued currency was redeemable for gold under the gold standard. The United States found itself diving directly into Phase 2 with both gold and silver currency, as well as paper representing precious metals and borrowing and lending facilities. A little over a century later, the Federal Reserve was established in 1913 after which the United States entered World War I, followed by the Roaring Twenties, and then the Great Depression. The catastrophic economic scenario would have led to central bank insolvency.

In 1933, to remediate this central bank fiasco, Franklin D. Roosevelt issued Presidential Proclamation 2039, which allowed the government to confiscate all gold and silver, including currency backed by the precious metals, and the Gold Reserve Act of January 30, 1934, included a change in the price of gold from $20.67 per troy ounce to $35, effectively increasing the money supply. During the next few decades, the United States was still settling international trade agreements using a gold-backed currency peg, and the dollar became the world reserve currency in 1944, which made it susceptible to **Triffin's paradox**.

Dollars were created and exported worldwide, and eventually, the dollars in circulation well outnumbered the gold that could back them. In 1971 after experiencing high inflation, the United States could no longer afford to swap the incoming dollars for gold, and it was at this time that the US dollar was declared fiat. Data from 1929 onward shows the US government debt has rarely increased by over $10 billion in any year, aside from the years during World War II when debts increased by amounts ranging from $58 billion to $64 billion in the years 1943, 1944, and 1945. However, after 1971, government debt in the United States took off, first breaking the World War II-era record for a single year in 1976 with $87 billion in additional debt, and then the single-year amount of new debt surpassed the $1 trillion mark in 2008, just one year after the launch of the iPhone, when the US housing market imploded due to speculative activity in the housing and mortgage-backed **securities** markets.

Less than a year prior to the 2008 housing meltdown, I moved to Chicago, iPhone in my pocket, and purchased a condo in Roscoe Village, just west of Wrigley Field. When the housing bust took down the economy, a large portion of equity in the condo disappeared in a flash. I was lucky to have a safe job in software development at the time and little in the form of investment capital in markets besides a couple of 401(k)s that contained relatively small amounts.

The Global Financial Crisis (GFC) would eventually sweep through the entire world economy and wipe out many banks, businesses, and individuals. But the story doesn't end predictably, with the insolvent banks going out of business and the fraudsters ending up in jail. In fact, exactly the opposite of this would play out in a series of bank bailouts. Using future taxpayer dollars to backstop their losses, the banks had socialized the risk but not before capitalizing on the rewards during the mania phase. This corrupt insider job between the revolving door of government regulators and banksters led to the social unrest and public demonstrations that became known as the Occupy Wall Street movement in 2011. Little did most of these protesters know that a potential answer to their problems was already set in motion on January 3, 2009, when a pseudonymous online persona known as Satoshi Nakamoto mined the Bitcoin **genesis block** with the following message embedded in the metadata portion: "The Times 03/Jan/2009 Chancellor on brink of second bailout for banks."

Humanity in 2009 was transitioning into the digital age with a smartphone soon to be in every pocket and with social media delivering endless memes that live deep down rabbit holes that only "the algorithm" knows how to navigate. The US government, for the first time in history, borrowed over a trillion dollars in one year, and a new form of money called

Bitcoin promised to become a new paradigm for Phase 1 money, a reflection of a profound virtual reality, appearing quietly in the ether of the internet.

CHAPTER 2

BITCOIN MECHANICS

Before the genesis block became the first block in the Bitcoin blockchain on January 3, 2009, the evolving digital age spawned many software enthusiasts, and many applications of software development were analogous to undiscovered territory yet to be explored. It took decades to develop the tools and resources that are necessary to fulfill the vision of Satoshi Nakamoto as described in the famous **white paper** titled, "Bitcoin: A Peer-to-Peer Electronic Cash System."* The abstract lays out how the system operates:

> Abstract. A purely peer-to-peer version of electronic cash would allow online payments to be sent directly from one party to another without going through a financial institution. Digital signatures provide part of the solution, but the main benefits are lost

---

* The Bitcoin white paper was originally published on October 31, 2008 by an individual or a group of people who called themselves Satoshi Nakamoto in a cryptography mailing list on a platform called Metzdowd. https://bitcoin.org/en/bitcoin-paper.

if a trusted third party is still required to prevent double-spending. We propose a solution to the double-spending problem using a peer-to-peer network. The network timestamps transactions by hashing them into an ongoing chain of hash-based proof-of-work, forming a record that cannot be changed without redoing the proof-of-work. The longest chain not only serves as proof of the sequence of events witnessed, but proof that it came from the largest pool of CPU power. As long as a majority of CPU power is controlled by nodes that are not cooperating to attack the network, they'll generate the longest chain and outpace attackers. The network itself requires minimal structure. Messages are broadcast on a best effort basis, and nodes can leave and rejoin the network at will, accepting the longest proof-of-work chain as proof of what happened while they were gone.

The system integrates solutions for two key problems that give the Bitcoin network the unique value proposition of having a high degree of decentralization and security.

The Byzantine generals problem (or Byzantine fault tolerance): In a peer-to-peer system, it is by design that there be no central source of truth, such as a database or command center because that would introduce one single point of failure or control. The key to resolving this issue is a consensus system among peers that is resilient to attacks or false information, such as repeated transactions or attempts to change the state of the accounting ledger.

A Bitcoin node consists of a copy of the ledger, including all transactional history, and an application that can verify each of the transactions is legitimate. The verification process relies on a data structure called the blockchain, named intuitively as the descriptor for a chain of blocks. A block in the blockchain serves the purpose of recording transactions, and the chain determines the sequence with which these transactions are processed, altogether representing the accounting ledger for the system at large. The sequence can easily and cheaply be verified by each node on the network. When a new block is created, it is broadcast in a peer-to-peer fan-out fashion until most nodes have verified it, cementing its place at the top of the chain. It is important to point out that the blockchain does not have much value if it's centrally controlled since in that case, it might as well be thought of as an inefficient database in a central command center. The value of the blockchain is derived from its use as a tool to solve the Byzantine generals problem, which is concerned with distributing the responsibility of verification widely in the network and minimizing the power of any one actor in the system, ideally maximizing decentralization without compromising security and reliability.

PROOF OF WORK

Similar to how gold must be mined to add to its total usable supply, Bitcoin is mined using computational power in exchange for securing the network. The decision to require energy and computational power to produce new Bitcoin blocks is one of the most debated aspects of blockchain technology, and there are other solutions with varying trade-offs. Requiring energy to be consumed to mine newly minted coins produces an incentive structure that maximizes system security while also fairly randomizing the distribution of the block reward. Additionally, scarcity is built into the system by applying an immutable limit of 21 million total coins, and the emission rate is based on the creation of new blocks that contain the mining reward. The target time to generate a new block is ten minutes, and a built-in difficulty adjustment makes sure that more computational power added to the overall system causes a counterbalanced change to the probability of generating a new block per hash.

As Bitcoin became more valuable, it incentivized the development of more powerful technologies that could compute the SHA-256 hashing function. Early mining could be successful on CPUs but eventually migrated to GPUs, which were orders of magnitude faster, and then finally application-specific integrated circuits (ASICs), which are chips designed specifically to compute SHA-256 hashes as efficiently as possible. This progression led to difficulty adjustments that kept the block emission rate close to the ten-minute target, regardless of overall hashing power.

At the time of this writing, the overall hash rate in the Bitcoin network is about 200 million TH/s. That's a two with twenty zeros, or 200,000,000,000,000,000,000 hashes per second. This network of miners is the most powerful distributed computational system on our planet, and it would require outpacing it to threaten the security of the Bitcoin ledger.

When Satoshi launched the Bitcoin network, it was the culmination of integrating these solutions, along with many of the technological developments produced during the digital age, that led to where we are today, and there is arguably a long way to go from here. Some compare the cryptocurrency asset space to the dot-com arena which started in a similar fashion, with an unhealthy dose of speculation and liberal funding of many companies that no longer exist today. The internet industry is still arguably in its infancy given that the internet was only popularized in the mainstream with the advent of easy-to-use mobile internet devices. We've only just discovered fire, but what will we do with it now as innovators determine new use cases for these nascent tools?

BITCOIN HALVINGS

"The Halvening" as it is sometimes called is an event that occurs when 210,000 blocks are added to the Bitcoin blockchain, and it is when the block's mining reward gets cut in half. When Bitcoin first launched, each block awarded the miner fifty newly minted bitcoin. The first halving reduced this reward to twenty-five, roughly four years later in 2013, then to 12.5 in 2016, and 6.25 in 2020. By reducing the mining reward in this manner, the emission rate logarithmically decreases over time. This means it reduces quickly in the beginning and then diminishes to a smaller and smaller decrease every 210,000 blocks until the reward eventually becomes zero after the total supply reaches the hard limit of 21 million total BTC. This emission rate emulates the physical process of discovery that emerges when harvesting a scarce asset given the diminishing nature of the emission rate. For example, at the beginning of the gold rush in California, a forty-niner, as they were called in 1849, would have mined hefty quantities of untapped gold reserves. With the passage of time, the easiest-to-acquire gold was mined, leaving a more difficult job to acquire the same amount when expending the same amount of time and effort. This process causes a logarithmic regression in the discovery rate and an exponential increase in the difficulty to acquire the same amount of the resource.

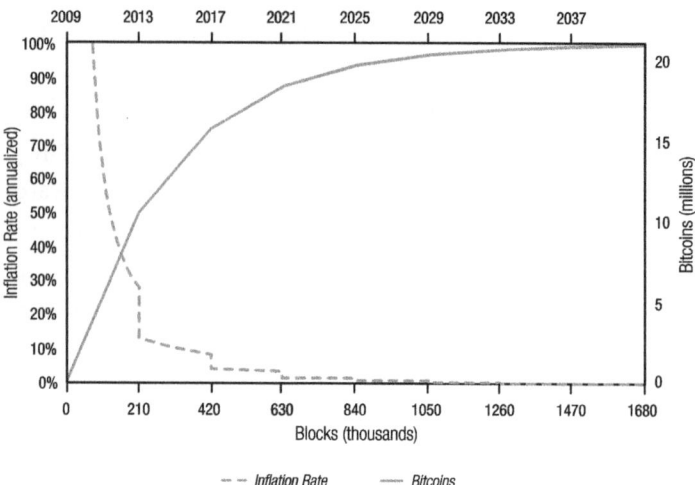

Figure 5

The ratio of the total existing usable supply, divided by the additionally created supply over a fixed time is called the **stock-to-flow ratio**, which typically is determined on a yearly basis. For gold today, roughly 2 percent of the supply is mined each year, which results in a stock-to-flow of around fifty, but it depends on the year and how much can be produced relative to the total supply. The calculation is relatively simple since it's the stock, or 100 percent of the asset, divided by the flow of newly discovered supply. One hundred percent divided by 2 percent is fifty, and this is a high stock-to-flow relative to other assets that have the properties of money. The stock-to-flow ratio represents scarcity and the difficulty level required to reduce scarcity over time. Bitcoin will have a much higher stock-to-flow than gold in the next halving slated for 2024 given that the stock is near 20 million and flow will be 3.125 per block (or 164,250 BTC per year) after the next halving. This results in a stock-to-flow of 20 million divided by 164,250 BTC per year created by miners, or a stock-to-flow of over 120. No other monetary asset on earth or in the human harvestable universe is anywhere near this stock-to-flow ratio. In other words, Bitcoin will be the scarcest and hardest-to-produce money after the halving event in 2024.

STORING BITCOIN

The term "**wallet**" is used as a metaphor, much like the term "desktop" is used to describe a computer's graphical user interface. A wallet application is software that can generate and help to secure/store **private-public key pairs** and, in most cases, provides a user interface to make the management of funds more convenient. The Bitcoin Core wallet available at bitcoin.org is an open source, free-to-use application built for Linux, macOS, and Windows operating systems. There are also mobile wallets available for smartphones from many software shops that provide various features and services integrations.

There are two basic types of wallets to consider depending on the user's needs, and they are light vs. full. To understand the difference between light and full wallets, it is necessary to understand what a **full node** is. A full Bitcoin node stores the full blockchain that is agreed on by the network to be the one and only legitimate chain going all the way back to the genesis block. Because the node maintains the full ledger, it is also able to verify pending transactions, and it can directly communicate new transactions to the network. A full node requires more computational and storage resources to operate. Roughly 300 GB of disk space is required to safely store the current Bitcoin blockchain at the time of writing, but this number will increase over time as new blocks are created.

Processing new transactions is also a growing function with the number of users actively transacting funds. There are off-the-shelf systems that provide enough RAM, CPU, and networking speeds to maintain a full node, such as the Casa Node 2. There are also do-it-yourself (DIY) projects with instructions on how to create a full node with a PC or a Raspberry Pi. Running a full node is the best way to be fully integrated into the network and to be positive that the wallet activity is directly interacting with other nodes on the network.

Running a light wallet delegates the transaction broadcasting to other full nodes on the network. For example, using a mobile light wallet, a transaction is created locally on the smartphone, and then typically the transaction data will be sent to a central service that runs the full nodes and finally broadcasts it on the main peer-to-peer network. The service is usually operated by the wallet developer and must be trusted to handle the transaction properly.

ACQUIRING BITCOIN

In the early days after the initial Bitcoin launch, obtaining Bitcoin was limited to a few options. Much of the early supply was mined using CPUs and GPUs before ASICs took over the mining space. There were also "faucets" that provided free Bitcoin to anyone curious to get onboarded with the new currency. People who owned Bitcoin would often send some to friends and/or family to get them started experimenting with the new technology, and posters on the BitcoinTalk forums would often include a donation address in their signature below each post. This allowed fans to contribute to online personas that helped with technical issues or general questions on various topics. Some businesses at the time accepted Bitcoin as payment for goods and services, but they were very few and far between in the early days.

The most common method of acquiring digital assets today is through an **exchange** such as Binance, Huobi, KuCoin, Coinbase, Kraken, and many more. In the early years, there was no well-defined regulatory framework for digital assets. Today, exchanges will typically require identification and bank account information to follow KYC/AML (know your customer/anti-money laundering) laws. Some exchanges are regulated by location to limit trading activity to specific regions. For example, Kraken is not available in the state of Washington, and exchanges in other countries sometimes block IP addresses from certain regions.

There are also peer-to-peer exchanges that use automated escrows such as LocalBitcoins, which allow people to trade fiat for digital currency directly. Another option for cash-to-crypto exchange that requires a bit more physical activity but is becoming more and more available are automated teller machines (ATMs), which will accept cash and scan wallet QR codes to transfer Bitcoin and other assets to a public address. Coinatmradar.com is a website where ATMs can be located, and it currently tracks over 38,000 ATMs.

Mining cryptocurrency is also a common method for acquiring various digital assets. Although Bitcoin and other SHA-256-based assets now require ASICs to achieve a meaningful share of the hash rate, some assets still use GPU-optimized hashing algorithms. The world of mining is a complex subject that could be the topic of many books on its own, and the industry players that run large-scale mining operations are typically well funded and well staffed. For example, Riot Blockchain and Marathon are publicly traded companies, and both have multibillion-dollar market caps as of this writing. In 2021, Riot had over 300 employees. This doesn't mean that entering the game requires a large-scale operation, but typically the juice isn't worth the squeeze if cheap power utilized at scale can't be achieved. An individual can still buy an ASIC miner, such as the Bitmain Antminer S19 Pro for around $6,000 on Amazon. Prices for various models fluctuate with the volatility of the market and availability, which is often very limited for some models.

The power requirements for these machines are an inconvenience for the average household, typically requiring 220-volt outlets, high amperage, and potentially climate control capable of keeping the machine cool enough to operate normally. The noise emanating from these machines can also be a significant problem for lived-in households, so most of these units are used at dedicated mining facilities rather than the laundry room of one's house.

Profitability depends on power prices by kilowatt-hour, typically ranging from a few cents (US) up to tens of cents depending on the jurisdiction and utility company. Areas near the Columbia River in Washington and Oregon have some of the lowest electricity rates due to easy access to cheap hydropower, but a typical household will likely have a low-profit margin, making these machines as useful as a loud space heater in the winter if breaking even. Mining in the United States is also taxed as regular income, so it tends to complicate finances depending on the operation.

Getting paid in digital assets is yet another way to acquire Bitcoin and other cryptocurrencies. In the last couple of years, famous NFL athletes have decided to get portions of their salaries in Bitcoin including Aaron Rodgers, Tom Brady, and Odell Beckham Jr. There are companies that offer services that will automatically convert part of a paycheck to Bitcoin and transfer it to a wallet of choice, such as Strike, CashApp, and Coinbase. A business can also accept payments in Bitcoin or other digital assets using popular e-commerce and PoS (point-of-sale) systems. Coinbase Commerce, Strike, BitPay, and Crypto.com are all providing simple-to-integrate solutions to accept payments in digital assets. This allows businesses to take a portion of revenue in digital assets and use settings that allow the merchant to decide how much of the payment is converted to currency if they want to dial in a percentage that gets converted to fiat to avoid the risk of volatility. One more way to obtain digital assets is to accept them for items sold through Craigslist.com or other local marketplaces. Craigslist provides an easy-to-use, free method to post items for sale where the sellers and buyers agree on an exchange. When creating a post, the seller can check a box labeled "cryptocurrency ok" to indicate that Bitcoin is accepted as payment. When people use cryptocurrency directly, it typically avoids the need for a middle entity that takes fees for services and eliminates some counterparty risk. A wallet-to-wallet transaction is like passing cash between people directly and only requires a small miner fee to execute a transaction. With recent wallets utilizing Bitcoin's lightning networks, fees are diminishing to near zero, which should incentivize the use of Bitcoin payments further because the fees are highly competitive when compared to alternative payment rails.

CHAPTER 3

LIFE BEFORE BITCOIN

How I came to be enamored with the digital age and eventually Bitcoin is likely a typical story of many people in my generation. My intention in this chapter is to share enough of my background to illustrate my financial values/standing and my relationship with technology at the time when I discovered Bitcoin to lay out the trajectory one might have taken to enter this brave new world.

THE EARLY YEARS

I was the first of four as an at-home birth on Spaulding Avenue in northwest Chicago. My three sisters were all born roughly two years apart after that in a different location near Wrigley Field on the north side of Chicago, so my siblings and I are all technically '80s millennials. We grew up relatively low on the financial scale with my dad paying the bills as a painter and carpenter to support the family and a member of a Chicago blues band in the twilight hours during those years. My mom was training to become an internationally board-certified lactation consultant (IBCLC) and, eventually with four kids in the city, had plenty to juggle at home. Mom also worked as a teacher in our homeschooling program. Around the time I was seven years old, there must have been one too many near misses on the "L" train station platforms wrangling a bunch of crazy kids, causing the family to move down to the south suburbs near the rest of my mom's side of the family. She was one of four as well, who immigrated from Italy in the '60s as a child to Chicago Heights, which is known for being one of Al Capone's hideout cities during the Prohibition era.

When I arrived in the south suburbs of Chicago in the early '90s and the family stayed in a room on the top floor of my grandparents' house, it was a mixed experience of old-school Italian culture, with the typical suburban entertainment provided by video games, and the Chicago Bulls dynasty that I remember having a significant impact on the family. During the transition, we all shared the same room until we were able to find our own home, a three-bedroom, one-bathroom ranch-style abode. I didn't know any better what it meant to be lower class or poor at the time. I remember appreciating that the family was always eating freshly made pasta and homemade marinara with the tomatoes, basil, and garlic grown every season in the backyard. Nonna (Italian for grandma) was the de facto boss of the family. Not speaking much English but hardworking, she instilled the values of a close-knit family, comfort food, and a no-nonsense mentality that seems quite rare now in our postmodern times.

Like a simulacrum of a mountain town south of Rome, the basement of my grandparents' home was multipurposed as a laundry room, kitchen, dining hall, and wine cellar, complete with handmade sausages and hot chili peppers drying from strings attached to my grandfather's handmade shelves that contained jars of fermenting tomato sauce.

My dad, with some help from the family, was able to get a job as a janitor at the local high school where my mom and her siblings graduated years prior. It was here that he would be able to pick up old computers that the school was tossing out, such as the family's first home computer, a TRS-80 Model III, which is a RadioShack relic from 1980. My first computer programming experience was in BASIC on those machines, and there were also many programs on stacks of 5.25" floppies from the school's classes that claimed to be high school-level math apps, which I was able to complete well before high school. The learning experience from those programs is likely what accelerated my learning process toward becoming an engineer.

Being homeschooled meant that classes were somewhat fluid and amorphous including guitar, computers, and library day where we picked out books and played with computers and the early internet. I must have been about ten years old when my sisters and I lined up on the couch for a lecture on binary code as my dad became more interested in the subject of computer science. When my dad went back to school for a graduate degree in computer science, that was justification to obtain a more modern PC. It was Apple's offerings that appeared to be better in terms of usability for the family, so we ended up with a Performa 6220 CD, with a 1GB hard drive, 16 MB of RAM, and a 4x CD-ROM drive. We were one of the first families on the block to get on the internet with a 14.4k modem and AOL (America On-Line) service, quickly running through the free five hours offered in the mail. In those early years using the internet, I mostly created websites with links to my favorite video game demos and newsgroups and posted custom maps and custom physics models for Marathon, a Mac-only game by Bungie Software back when they were a two-bit outfit in Chicago before being acquired by Microsoft to launch the Halo series on Xbox.

When it came time to go to high school, I was already accelerated in math courses, taking high school-level algebra a grade early at Marian Catholic High, the local private high school, and this was where I wanted to go for a four-year high school program, but my parents weren't so sure given the high tuition. Being the first child means everything is a "trial run," and all choices come with heightened uncertainty for parents. The ultimatum I was given was to work for it and hand over my paychecks if I was going to be a financial burden on the family for my luxurious educational choices. Working to pay for school taught me a couple of things: (1) minimum wage at $4 per hour would mean a lot of work if I wanted to afford tuition, and (2) I would do anything possible not to end up working in manual labor as an adult.

WELCOME TO ADULTHOOD

By the time I graduated high school, my dad had also received his graduate degree in computer science, so it was during this time that the family really started to get serious about the digital age. My choice was to go to school for engineering, and two universities accepted my application: Purdue University and Bradley University. After visiting the campuses, I knew Bradley was going to be better for me, and my first two years in the electrical engineering program confirmed my choice. I had solid grades and a decent job in the work study program at the music department to help pay for things. I also had a summer job back home at the public school in Chicago Heights, wiring up the building with its first Ethernet network and building out their PC labs, where I learned to build custom machines running Linux or Windows, eventually leading to an interest in PC gaming and an obsession with tomshardware.com, following the recent trends in computer architectures, and video game rendering performance. My parents, along with some loans and scholarships, helped me through the initial phases. It was later in my junior year that things took an interesting turn.

In the summer of 2003, after my second year at Bradley, the lead singer in my band and I planned to rent an off-campus house with the vision of entertaining the student body on weekends with local music and all the Milwaukee's Best Lager a student could take down. We found a real "gem" at Cooper and Main Street, conveniently located a couple of blocks away from the engineering school, where we had most of our classes. With a third roommate, we could each pay as little as $275 per month to live the college dream at a place that I would compare to 537 Paper Street in my all-time favorite movie, *Fight Club*. Paint cracking off the walls, mold flourishing in a fractal pattern on the ceilings of the bathrooms, single-pane windows with their original wooden frames that leaked heat at the same rate the poor furnace could pump it out in the cold Illinois winters, and a basement that we nicknamed the Snake Hole (although no snakes helped us with the rat infestation). The house would be our headquarters for funding the rest of my undergrad education, which was now 100 percent my financial responsibility.

My twenty-first birthday party included four bands (including my own), five kegs of Milwaukee's Best Original Lager, and two five-gallon jugs of an elixir we called Jungle Juice consisting of a precisely measured mixture of Skol Vodka, red Kool-Aid mix, some freshly squeezed citrus, and ice water. Neon pink vomit splatter became a surprise work of modern art enjoyed every other Sunday morning at the Snake Hole. One roommate was in a fraternity, which meant that our guest list ballooned to the hundreds easily. With the power of a cell phone to mass text all our friends the schedule, we would go through about 200 cups, sometimes many more, at $5 each. We consistently threw these parties once every two weeks, with profits being reinvested toward paying the rent, better sound systems, keg equipment, and cleaning supplies that would be crucial. We had run-ins with the local police due to porch dwellers, so we learned to let everyone smoke inside. The cigarette ash embedded in the carpet would have to be extracted with an industrial vacuum cleaner, and the random vomit splatters (often found in the strangest places) would require industrial mopping gear and loads of herbal "incense" the day after these events. The first year at the off-campus house was incredibly exciting, and although our band wasn't that well tuned yet, we became better over time and consistently played shows at our Snake Hole and other venues in the area.

It was also an extremely challenging time financially. I had to sell one of my guitars at a certain point to cover the rent. I was on scholarships and a couple of government student loans with deferred interest, so school was mostly paid for besides books and other scholarly supplies, such as pencils, calculators, lab notebooks, and acceptable clothing to show up to class, but clothing often suffered as a backseat priority. The ripped knee holes in my jeans started as a fashion statement but a year later became an obvious "I'm broke" statement when the holes opened to full frontal shin views.

The budget to sustain living month to month in this situation required eating the same diet of peanut butter and jelly sandwiches, soups, grilled cheese, $1 pizzas, and on good days, grilled chicken with pasta. My total food budget was somewhere around $50 a week at the local Walmart, and the closest thing to craft beer I could afford was Rolling Rock at about $9 per twelve pack. My roommate would criticize me for being a beer snob, paying about $1 per bottle, while he opted for Hamm's twenty-four packs at $9 each, getting two times the beer for the money, but I have high standards when it comes to beer. My total annual burn rate was under $10,000, but even at this level of poverty, the biweekly parties were necessary to keep up with expenses, and we managed to consistently deliver.

Toward the end of the 2003–2004 school year, a series of events made it hard for me to imagine pushing forward to finish school. The class material reached peak difficulty levels that year with full-day labs and hypercomplex theory and mathematics, sometimes requiring all-night studying sessions. I was still motivated and interested in the subject matter, but the required studying and volume of homework after classes allowed for little free time and often very little sleep. I also knew that I'd have to finish within four years or face another rental cycle and the possibility of more tuition payments without sufficient loans or scholarships. It was a do-or-die situation in my mind after doing some basic budgeting. They say when it rains, it pours, and it was on a hot summer day that my truck wouldn't start. The starter was never perfectly reliable, but on this day, it decided to burst into flames. Paying to fix it nearly wiped me out, and by this time I was racking up revolving credit on a couple of cards and paying the minimum payments to squeak by. When the truck finally broke down for good in a CVS parking lot and I couldn't pay to get it towed, I left it parked in the lot after extracting the CDs and stereo. The truck remained parked there for a few days and finally disappeared. Later, I received a note from the local police explaining that the truck had been towed to an impound where it would be junked if I didn't claim it. I didn't have the money to support car ownership, and so I promptly threw the letter in the garbage pile, and that was that. Without a gas-powered vehicle in my possession, I'd have to walk my laundry down the street to Squeaky Clean since our washer/dryer at home didn't work.

Making matters even worse was the inability to return to a well-paying IT job in the summer, which led to working two odd jobs to pay the rent and get ready for the next school year. I worked in the electrical engineering lab as a technician, putting together lab benches and soldering parts for upcoming lab sessions. At night, I worked at a downtown bar called Babe's on Main Street as a door guy, checking IDs and restocking the bar before closing. The hours were brutal, but on some of the busier nights, I shared tips with the bartenders, which helped with the cash situation, and an occasional comped Budweiser as we closed around 5:00 a.m. usually helped me sleep in the daytime. The last year of school felt a lot easier after getting through the summer. After making sure tuition and work study programs were still in place with about half of my tuition paid in scholarships and the other half covered with new student loans, I could worry about studying and hosting epic parties to get me through the rest. When I started the program in the first year, over one hundred students were electrical engineering majors, and that number had dwindled to about thirty by graduation.

EARLY CAREER BUILDING

Education is an investment, and it's an expensive one depending on which school and how much financial support is offered through scholarships, government loans, and help from parents or other friends and family members. When I went to school, I didn't know this, nor did I even think about investments and money beyond budgeting for survival. The education system kept me in a mindset bubble where the only thing that mattered was getting the degree and somehow managing to sustain life for under $10,000 a year. Now with student loan debt and some revolving debt in credit cards, it would be necessary to find a job.

What I had been mostly distracted from this whole time during my college years was that the technology space was going through the dot-com crash, and just as I was graduating, the NASDAQ had recovered only about half of the total losses from its peak. Looking back on this, it's amazing how distracted I was from these economic events during school. The aftermath of the dot-com bubble bursting was now something I had to contend with as I finished school and attempted to enter the tech industry.

Entry-level jobs were scarce, and I was lucky enough to have a contact from school who was a teacher assistant in our labs. He was already a manager at a company called Belcan Engineering, doing contracts for Caterpillar R&D projects, primarily automating construction with embedded software and controls systems. I was thrilled to get the job and put my education to work in the professional arena making construction machines automatically dig holes, with the goal of also digging myself out of a financial hole. This became a turning point for me that would change my career trajectory significantly because at the time, I was mainly into hardware and subjects such as robotics, circuit design, and Simulink or MATLAB-based applications, but this job turned me on to the world of software development.

The project I started off with at Belcan included developing a touch-screen-based interface. This is what started me on a path that would eventually lead to a focus on UI/UX and various forms of front-end software development.

My interest in video games in conjunction with new experiences developing graphical interfaces and graphics software inspired me to go back to school for a graduate degree in software engineering. After a couple of years at Belcan, my girlfriend at the time graduated and did a study abroad program in France. But when she returned, the only jobs available for her were in Chicago, so we decided to move to the big city where I had lived for several of my early years.

    I took this change as an opportunity to apply for graduate school and was accepted into DePaul University's program with a concentration in video games and graphics. Compared to today, very few schools at the time offered any video game programs, and the mobile phone sector was still fighting to go mainstream with the iPhone just on the horizon in 2007. Living through this time as a technology enthusiast was incredibly productive. Coming out of the 2001 crash meant that most bubble-phase projects had been wiped out, and what remained was a lean set of companies competing for what would become a software- and internet-driven future. Web 2.0 was maturing with the rise of cloud computing, social media, and the ability for users to create content with an online identity, bringing a fresh wave of growth to the internet industry.

    I was back in school mostly taking classes at DePaul's downtown School of Technology, but I'd soon run out of money to fund the endeavor. DePaul and Chicago in general required a change in mindset over finances. I took out a private loan from Chase at a 6 percent interest rate, putting me in a deeper financial hole, but I was so confident that this was what I needed to do at the time to achieve my goals, so I looked at the expenses as an investment. As my software skills grew at a healthy pace, my finances continued to suffer, so I started looking for a software job. I was at a disadvantage to do this before finishing the graduate degree in software engineering. My résumé was more geared toward hardware development at the time, and employers were thrown off by my lack of applicable software experience. That didn't stop WMS Gaming (formerly Williams) from giving me a shot at an associate software engineering role—the entry-level software developer position.

WMS was started by Stanford graduate and entrepreneur Harry Williams in 1943 as a pinball machine company but later evolved to be an innovator in the video slot machine industry. I started working on their games, including titles such as *Diamonds of Dublin* and *3-Alarm Fire*. Between working on games for the slot machine industry and learning software fundamentals at school, this was a time of accelerated learning and building the self-confidence to become a more respected software developer.

A most welcome perk was that the company would end up paying for most of my classes, which I was taking at night after work and mostly remotely from a home office. In those early days of remote learning, web-based apps with tiny pixelated videos and a live whiteboard would have been laughable by today's standards, but I got by. It was during this time when I also started to deliver my own iPhone apps on the App Store.

My first app, Locket, was almost the first to market of its kind, but by the time it shipped, there was already an iLocket and many more clones followed. The top ten apps at the time included novelty gimmicks such as a Zippo lighter app and iBeer, which was a beer-drinking simulator that involved gesturing the phone as if it were a mug to elicit a pouring animation on the screen. The clever novelty of this app supposedly earned the developer riches in the millions of dollars, which seemed absurd but also stoked the masses to deliver many more kitschy apps.

AWAKENING TO THE IMPORTANCE OF POLITICS AND ECONOMICS

One of the issues with being so caught up in these interest bubbles is that other important aspects of life are easy to ignore, and for me, the economy was one of those blind spots. I was able to take a break from programming in the office to witness the presidential election victory speech given by Barack Obama in Grant Park, which was one of the most celebrated events based on the collective attitude of thousands of victorious participants. However, shortly after this, the sitting president, George W. Bush, killed the party when announcing that there was another financial disaster in the works ready to unravel in the following months: the 2008 GFC, which came all too soon for many people who were still pulling themselves out of the 2001 dot-com fiasco.

I remember how easy it was to get approved for a home loan in 2008. As a first-time home buyer with loads of student debt and my girlfriend being the breadwinner with her new teaching job, we were somehow easily able to get an approval letter for up to a $300,000 home loan without filling out any paperwork, allowing us to buy our condo at the top of the market. The economy was destroyed when millions of people defaulted on mortgages, and banks such as Lehman Brothers had supported much of their balance sheet with the mortgage-backed securities that bundled the overrated mortgages into a poisonous financial product.

I had very little understanding of what was happening due to my lack of knowledge regarding economics, housing, and derivative assets. I still had my job, but there were layoffs and cutbacks sweeping through the economy. Midway Games, the creators of the *Mortal Kombat* series, which was right next door to my office at WMS, filed for bankruptcy in 2009, and a few of their employees came to join us in the more recession-resilient gambling industry. With the condo nearly underwater and my stack of debts, all I could do was keep grinding, and I eventually moved up from associate to core level and then to senior software engineer during the time the government bailouts were passed by Congress to avoid the "too big to fail" bank implosion.

In a fiat-based world, creating new money is easy. New debt can be taken out to service old debts, and the Federal Reserve is an infinite buyer of last resort. I may not have understood what a bailout was if it hadn't been for a new form of money I didn't know about yet, one that quietly entered the arena in 2009 aiming to offer an alternative currency native to the internet.

It was in a casual conversation during a family get-together later in 2011 that my dad brought up Bitcoin, a mysterious cryptographically secure digital money. It took new technology with the promise of **sound money principles** for me to get interested in understanding these political and economic concepts, and it all started with a simple dinner conversation.

PART II

THE BITCOIN CYCLES

CHAPTER 4

CYCLE 1

BEACON SIGNAL

The technology space is always bustling with new developments, and when Bitcoin was capturing a modest audience in 2009, it was mostly through organic growth leveraging internet engagement to gain adoption and network effects. It was when the price of Bitcoin rallied from $0 to a little above $30 that journalists in more prominent media outlets raised awareness of the new experimental internet currency, and the word eventually found its way to me via my dad who must have randomly found news about it in his internet feed in the summer of 2011.

Euphoric price action acts as a beacon signal and brings new players into the market when the news goes viral. Today, a significant portion of the internet-connected population is aware of Bitcoin, but back in 2011, a vast majority hadn't yet heard of it. Later when I was at my home office, I did a quick search and easily found the famous Bitcoin white paper by Satoshi Nakamoto on the bitcoin.org domain. The perfect storm of events leading to this moment can't be overstated. My story, which I assume to be very relatable to many other millennials, was one of financial hardship personally but also of volatile ups and downs in market boom-and-bust cycles causing heightened uncertainty and financial turmoil for many people.

This period was one of great distress, culminating in the Occupy Wall Street movement, and the news cycle was gushing with financial terminology I had never heard before. My curiosity led me down the financial rabbit hole, watching YouTube and reading articles for hours about modern banking, fiat currency, gold, quantitative easing, and how Bitcoin fits into the global economic equation. The thesis driving Bitcoin enthusiasts at the time was a bet on fiat monetary inflation artificially expanding the money supply and the need for an asset with a limited supply to hedge against the irresponsibility of the institutions in charge. Unlike gold, Bitcoin was digitally secured and verified with every public address having a balance on the open ledger.

Until Bitcoin was invented, the digital world was known to provide the opposite of scarcity: cheap copies of data, which disrupted existing business models such as anything printed on paper, and digital physical media of all kinds that could be copied and distributed widely using decentralized protocols like **BitTorrent**. Bitcoin introduced scarcity and decentralized consensus, requiring no central authority to manage the ledger. The major hurdle Bitcoin would have to overcome at the time was adoption, which was initially hindered by a significant technical barrier to entry for the average investor and nearly impossible at the time for any institution responsible for large quantities of investable capital due to the absence of legal frameworks/regulations of any kind existing for the new asset class. To put this in perspective, it was like a financial instrument from another galaxy had landed on earth and became immediately operational before more than a handful of people could even figure out how it worked.

Still to this day in 2023, there is a lack of regulatory clarity on digital asset investing, and the debate over which digital assets should be regulated by the Securities and Exchange Commission (SEC) as securities are still often debated in the community. On top of the financial reasons to get interested in Bitcoin at the time, there was also a fascinating technical component that drew me in as an up-and-coming engineer in the field of software. I spent hours trying to understand the math and reasoning behind Satoshi's new technology. I didn't have any idea at the time if adoption would reach significant levels, but the built-in profit incentive to contribute to the security of the network and the supply dynamics being modeled after the extraction of a rare earth metal like gold made a lot of sense, and I needed no convincing that the internet was already on its way to mainstream success.

It became clear to me that Bitcoin was something worth getting involved in, and gaining some hands-on experience was the next step. It wasn't long before I figured out how to fund a Mt. Gox account and make a Bitcoin purchase, but at the time, exchanges weren't nearly as mature as they are today. First, it wasn't certain that Mt. Gox or any other exchange would be reliable, and there were no guarantees or backstops in this new Wild West of a market.

Exchange services were unreliable and risky in terms of the legal framework for digital assets at the time being nonexistent. The first step was getting money from Chase to Mt. Gox, which involved e-commerce middleware I had never heard of called Dwolla. When I decided to commit to a BTC purchase on Mt. Gox, I gave myself 50/50 odds that it would work and I'd see any of the money again, so I had to tread carefully. After days of settling funds with Dwolla, the balance finally showed up in my Mt. Gox account. So I went in and bought all the BTC I could with $1,000, snagging roughly 65 BTC at around $15 each. Then it was a matter of withdrawing the Bitcoin balance and sending it to my Bitcoin Core wallet, which fortunately worked as expected.

MY FIRST PURCHASE USING BITCOIN

Exchanging fiat money for Bitcoin was the first accomplished step, but this was only the beginning of the learning experience. I was already aware of a few mentions on the BitcoinTalk forums of merchants accepting Bitcoin as payment, but this was something I needed to try for myself to prove that Bitcoin was really a form of money and not just a collectible token to speculate on.

Looking around on YouTube, there were a few unboxing videos showing packages with products that were supposedly purchased with Bitcoin, such as wool socks. I ended up choosing a merchant called Bitjerky, which sold boxes of either regular or spicy beef jerky for Bitcoin directly on the website. I can no longer find any references to the service, but it was a very simple site, and I remember the merchant was operating out of a cattle ranch in Nevada. I chose a pound of spicy Bitjerky for 1.1 BTC, worth about $17 at the time, which included shipping to Chicago. The public address with the amount to send showed up in the checkout process and I opened the Bitcoin Core wallet to promptly send the payment. An email confirmed that the payment had been received and the order was being processed. A few days later, I received the box containing what would be the most expensive beef jerky I've eaten to date, given that the 1.1 BTC is now worth tens of thousands of dollars, but the experience was valuable, and the jerky was pretty good too.

BUILDING A BITCOIN MINER

I was feeling pretty good about Bitcoin's blockchain technology as a form of money after successfully using it to make a purchase, but the learning process didn't stop there. I was running the Bitcoin Core wallet with a fully synced node, so I was able to watch the transactions and trace the balance to previous transactions on the blockchain. As new transactions flowed through my node and new blocks appeared on the chain, I grew more curious about mining these blocks, and I had a basic sense of how people were minting new Bitcoin at a rate of fifty BTC approximately every ten minutes with each new block, so I thought I'd give it a try.

There were many helpful threads in the community forums that explained procedures to start mining, and after a few command line entries on my MacBook Pro, I was able to kick off a CPU miner, with the fans in the laptop whirring wildly to suck heat away from the core components. Doing a bit more research, I realized that GPU miners were coming online, causing the difficulty of mining new blocks to go up and therefore making it improbable that my CPU would be capable of producing a new block.

I left the machine running for about one day without any luck, and the mining software made it difficult to use other apps due to overwhelming the CPU for hash power. Doing some more research, I realized I could probably make a profit with a GPU miner based on electricity costs. I picked up a Frankenstein PC sitting in my dad's home office with a decent CPU and enough RAM and disk space for a full Bitcoin node. The remaining key ingredient to install was the GPU, which I grabbed from a local PC store. There were websites with tables listing GPUs and their corresponding hash rates on the Bitcoin forums, and AMD GPU architectures were better for generating

SHA-256 hashes, which meant much more hash power for the cost per unit.

After some research, I found a decent GPU for around $200 and installed it in the PC's open PCI Express slot. Then I installed Ubuntu Linux and followed some instructions on the forums to get the miner started. I signed up for a mining pool, which spreads out the hashing work among other miners in the pool, paying a portion of the earnings from new blocks based on the share of hashes I produced as a contribution to the block among the other pool participants. After a bit of troubleshooting and configuration file modifications, it all worked as expected! With a little bit of extra noise and heat in the home office, I was in business mining shares of new Bitcoin with a pool. About a month later, the mining pool dashboard stats indicated that the PC was pulling in somewhere between five and ten BTC on about $40 per month of electricity costs, which was barely profitable at 2012 Bitcoin prices.

All of this was plenty of fun until the bear market of 2012 sucked the wind out of the sails of the community, and it was no less brutal than any recent Bitcoin bear market. The price receded to a low of $2 only a couple of months later, putting me in the hole on my original investment by about 86 percent. In dollar terms, this was like going from $1,000 down to $140. This loss was a large one for me at the time given that I still had plenty of loans to pay off, and it might seem like this should have been the buying opportunity of a lifetime in hindsight. However, even though I was tempted to dump my 401(k) and go all into the new asset class, there were also a lot of dark narratives pulling down my conviction.

I remember watching videos of Max Keiser and Peter Schiff having completely opposite views with Keiser having the emphatic bull case, whereas Schiff was convinced that Bitcoin would die off and be known as the next tulip bubble craze, referencing the famous Dutch frenzy over perishable flowers in 1636. Some of it made sense to me, but a lot of it didn't, so the result was more confusion than anything. In the end, I didn't make any significant investment decisions when the price hit the bottom. I guess I could say I was "in it for the tech" above all else. Some people on the forums were convinced that Bitcoin was dead for good, and this was followed by a barrage of articles that would later be collected on the Bitcoin obituary archive. I would later learn that this volatility acted more like a feature than a bug because it is exactly what brought me and so many others into the space.

BEAR MARKET BLUES

Bitcoin and finance became a new hobby for me on top of the existing stack of responsibilities: a full-time job, finishing grad school, and a new startup concept to make iPhone apps for local businesses. Going into my late twenties, all this work was taking a toll on my health and taking a larger toll on relationships, including the one that mattered most at the time.

It's interesting how living with a person doesn't guarantee a healthy relationship or that two lives will continue on a shared path without commitment to maintaining shared goals. I was spending most of my time in a portal, through a screen, keyboard, and mouse, where endless technological advancements were taking place and capturing most of my mental cycles. I didn't realize that this degree of separation was causing the surrounding physical world to fade into the background until my partner in life decided to leave.

This breakdown of the eight-year relationship makes sense now, but back then, I was blindsided by it. This shocking turn of events derailed a few things that ended up changing my trajectory as I neared the age of thirty. One change was that I ended up moving out of the condo, which dismantled my office situation. When I moved into a new apartment, my interest in setting up the same working environment gave me pause because it reminded me of being a techno addict. I did not want to restart the home office operation just yet, and instead of working side jobs as an iPhone developer and tinkering with Bitcoin, I put those things down for a while and focused on my full-time job where I'd recently been promoted to a lead role.

With my graduate degree now complete, I wouldn't have to worry about doing online classes or homework in a dedicated home office, so I didn't bother setting up my PC miner either. I sold most of my Bitcoin to consolidate finances and split them down the middle with the ex. When all was said and done, I decided to pay off my student debt instead of investing more in assets, and my remaining balance in Bitcoin was around 3.6 BTC in late 2012 when the price had rebounded from the 2012 lows to over $10 in the third quarter that year.

It's amusing to note that if I had simply held on to the original 65 BTC and done nothing else, it would be valued at $1,300,000 at today's current price of around $20,000. But at the all-time high as of this writing at $69,000, it would have been worth over $4,000,000. Hindsight is always 20/20 when it comes to investing, so I try not to beat myself up over this. It's all part of the learning experience, and it played a valuable role in my decision-making over the years. I value the learning experiences more than the money that came and went because of managing my own investments.

Learning and growth have not only come in the form of more prudent investment practices and a better understanding of economics and markets but also in the form of growing with the digital assets space by participating in learning about all the ideas and innovations driving its advancement with hands-on experience. In these early years, when Bitcoin was the only publicly used blockchain in existence, I knew that it was something worth exploring further, but I could have never predicted where the digital asset space was headed.

CHAPTER 5

CYCLE 2

THE FIRST HALVING

On November 28, 2012, I was living through the beginnings of one of the coldest Chicago winters on record when the first Bitcoin halving brought the mining block reward down from 50 BTC to 25 BTC. This transition, which is firmly coded in the Bitcoin protocol, doubled the stock-to-flow ratio of Bitcoin. With a total supply of about 10.5 million at the time and a block emission rate of one block containing 25 BTC per ten minutes, this meant the flow was halved to 1,314,000 BTC per year. The lower emission rate meant that a miner who aimed to be profitable would now earn half as much Bitcoin for the same hash rate and thus see revenue in Bitcoin cut in half, assuming the same hash rate is maintained. This dynamic in isolation is not necessarily a predictor of Bitcoin's price action, but it plays a crucial role in what many market participants would define as a new cycle for Bitcoin.

There are other factors when it comes to the intra-cycle

price action, and one of those major factors is adoption, which drives the network effects per Metcalfe's law. Growth in the space exploded with the number of transactions going from under 10,000 per day in early 2012 to over 100,000 over the next three years. The price for 1 BTC ascended soon after the halving in 2013 from about $13 in January to $231 in April, representing an increase of about 1,600 percent.

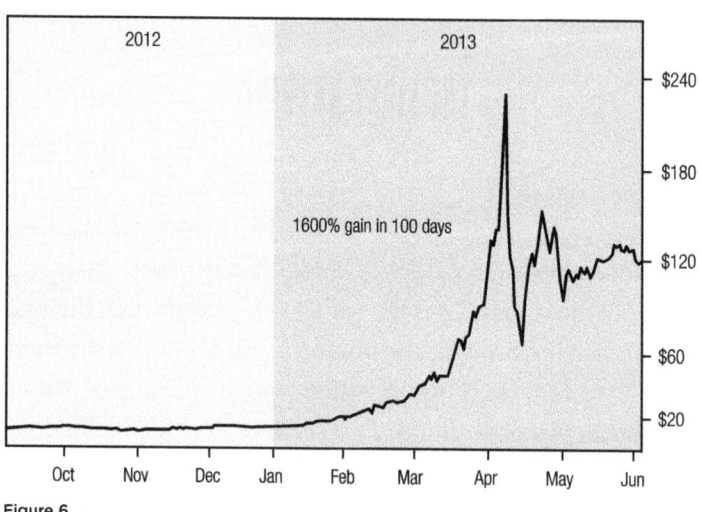

Figure 6

During the initial price takeoff in 2013, I was distracted from Bitcoin news due to focusing on increased responsibilities as a manager at work and settling into an unfamiliar mode of single life at my new apartment. I had successfully paid off all debts and made an effort to balance out my lifestyle by adding some gym time to my routine and getting back into performing music at local open mic shows.

A few months passed before a familiar conversation started

between me and a coworker as I was asked, "Have you heard of Bitcoin?" The news cycle picked up on the recent price action, and by this time there were some debates regarding the future of Bitcoin between pundits on networks like CNBC, which seemed a bit surreal because I was never sure in the early days if Bitcoin would ever grow to be a part of the mainstream conversation. Based on the narrative in conversations on CNBC, it was obvious that the world of finance hadn't done the research to fully understand why Bitcoin's price was moving upward and outpacing every other asset class. They hadn't the slightest clue what gave it any value since there was no physical representation whatsoever, which was certainly amusing to watch but also humbling because I realized that I should do my own diligence to challenge the belief systems I had taken for granted in the past. What gives Bitcoin value remains to be one of the most interesting debates, and the conversation evolves, eliciting new perspectives and insights as more proponents face off with ardent naysayers.

Because I worked in the software field and was surrounded by technically inclined engineers in my day-to-day life, it was straightforward for me to discuss the ins and outs of Bitcoin and my experience with it leading up to the new buzz that captured more participants. I became a local, early go-to resource on the subject because I had friends who were now interested in mining and using Bitcoin, and they found value in discussing my direct experience with exchanges, wallets, and mining.

As the word spread around the office, I would have regular conversations with coworkers regarding their experience with all things Bitcoin, but one conversation stood out and I remember quite vividly where I was introduced to **altcoins**. An "alt," as they are often called, was a term given to any digital blockchain asset that was not Bitcoin. Given that the core source code was under an open-source license, a software developer could easily copy the protocol, wallet software, and any other components necessary to start a new blockchain-based asset.

We discussed a few coins including Dark Coin (which later became Dash), Litecoin, and Dogecoin. I remember being at the office pulling up the original Dogecoin YouTube promo video, which featured the now famous Shiba Inu mascot piloting a rocket in one scene, then, with a hard hat and pickax, mining shiny coins in a cave. I laughed it off and didn't even consider investing in any of these for a second, proclaiming that the idea of a Bitcoin clone seemed more like a scam than a legitimate project. At the time, I wasn't really that interested in diving deep into other cryptocurrency projects, but I was curious to watch this play out from the sidelines with my small investment in BTC still locked up in **cold storage**, safely secured using an encrypted disk image containing the wallet.dat file, not to be found on any machine connected to the internet. This was a time before Trezor, Ledger, or any other hardware wallet solutions existed and wallet. dat files were unencrypted, plain text, with the public-private key pairs exposed so that the wallet software could import a user's history and cryptographically sign transactions.

I'd occasionally check in with the same coworkers who were now getting very hyped up as the price action continued to soar in 2013. Toward the end of the year, Bitcoin had reached $1,000 for the first time and complete euphoria had set in for people who were actively buying and mining new coins. Like the beacon signal that brought me into the fold in 2011, 2013's peak Bitcoin price of $1,242 recorded by Mt. Gox elicited a wave of excitement that pulled in many new investors. It was the new paradigm phase of the Cycle 2 bubble. A headline from *The Guardian* from Monday, November 25, 2013 read, "Is Bitcoin About to Change the World?"

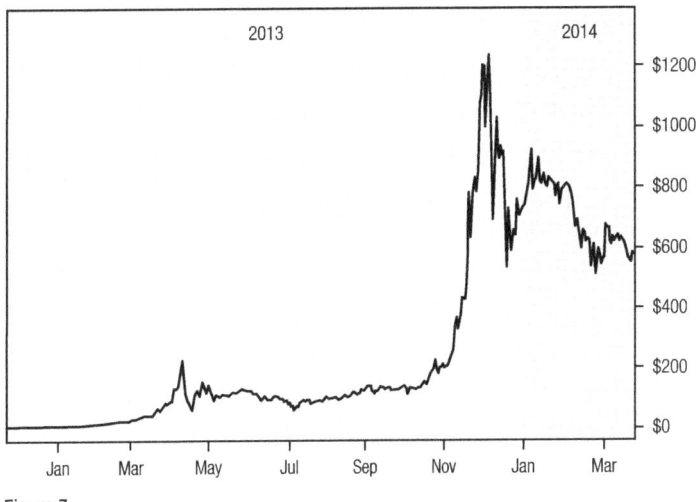

Figure 7

While everyone seemed to be happy with their gains at the end of 2013 and imagined a future where cryptocurrency would take over the legacy banking system, there were two major disasters developing in the shadows that would change the minds of many advocates and provide plenty of ammo for the nonbelievers to validate their stance that crypto was a scam all along. The stories of the Silk Road drug cartel and the Mt. Gox meltdown became the defining pivotal events that led to the next bear market rout.

SILK ROAD

Transaction privacy was never a promise that Satoshi Nakamoto claimed in the original Bitcoin white paper, yet the narrative that Bitcoin transactions were private emerged due to addresses on the blockchain not being considered traceable to personally identifiable information. A Bitcoin public address is a string of characters that can be tracked in the publicly accessible blockchain, but creating a wallet with new public-private key pairs doesn't require a sign-up process where personal information is required; they are simply generated by a wallet application.

The illusion of anonymity developed into an assumed value proposition for Bitcoin as a payment network in black markets where illicit products and services were offered. The most popular illegal marketplace during the 2013 Bitcoin bull run was Silk Road, a website that was hidden behind an onion routing system called Tor, which made it difficult to trace client activity on the sites that existed on the "dark web." The Silk Road marketplace offered a wide range of products and accepted Bitcoin as payment. Using an escrow to hold funds until transactions were finalized and then taking a commission from each purchase, Silk Road's operation could take in revenue without posting and selling products of its own. It was effectively an eBay or Amazon marketplace that connects vendors to buyers but for the purpose of handling illegal product exchanges that a regulated company couldn't offer. Product offerings included illegal drugs, steroids, stimulants, and many more illicit items. An estimated $15 million per year in transactions were processed, and a total of 614,305 BTC in commissions were collected by the site before it was stopped by the FBI in October 2013.

Bitcoin's transparent public blockchain was potentially the key to Silk Road's eventual downfall. The details haven't been fully disclosed by the FBI or the IRS investigators, but it is known that involvement by one of the first blockchain analysis companies, Chainalysis, aided in the seizure of Silk Road's Bitcoin. Chainalysis uses metadata and patterns of behavior along with complex algorithms to determine relationships between blockchain accounts and the people who utilize them. It's a sophisticated system that makes an openly accessible blockchain like Bitcoin's unreliable for anonymous activity, and yet still to this day, Bitcoin is haunted by the reputation of being a payment system designed for black market activity, partly because of the history of Silk Road. Rumors sprang from the news of the seizure, implying that Bitcoin had security flaws added to the destruction of confidence in the reliability of blockchain to secure monetary assets, further convincing people that Bitcoin didn't have a future and was soon to be dead and gone forever (again). Of course, these rumors were later proven to be misleading, but the reputational damage could not be undone so easily.

MT. GOX

In 2006, a programmer named Jed McCaleb decided to create a website for exchanging Magic: The Gathering Online cards. McCaleb purchased the domain name mtgox.com in early 2007 and launched a beta version of the site but then lost interest in maintaining it and moved on to other projects. In 2010, McCaleb first read about Bitcoin and realized that there was a need for an exchange where fiat currency could be traded for the new decentralized asset, and the Bitcoin exchange was live by July 18 of the same year. As Bitcoin's price and number of users rose sharply, it became apparent that the site would have to scale to handle the rising traffic and trading volume, but McCaleb didn't want to continue to develop and scale the operation of Mt. Gox, so it was sold to a French developer named Mark Karpeles on June 13, 2011.

As the Bitcoin price increased in Cycle 2, hackers became more incentivized to exploit weaknesses in the exchange. Around the same time that Cycle 1 was peaking at over $30 per Bitcoin, exploits allowed 25,000 BTC to be stolen, and a separate hack into the account of an exchange auditor allowed someone to sell the exchange's holdings on the market. Despite numerous instabilities and exploits, the site grew in popularity, handling over 70 percent of all Bitcoin trades by 2013, including my first buy order in 2011 and a sell order when I sold off most of my holdings going into Cycle 2 in 2012. Because I was going through a swirl of changes in my life that distracted me from Mt. Gox and keeping the small amount of Bitcoin I had in cold storage, I was lucky enough to stay out of what would become an epic disaster around the time Cycle 2 peaked in December 2013. Mt. Gox started to report issues clearing deposits.

In the November 2013 issue of *Wired* magazine, it was reported that customers were waiting weeks to months for cash withdrawals from Mt. Gox to execute. Cycle 2 reached the euphoria phase as the price of Bitcoin reached a high of $1,240 on December 5, and on February 4, 2014, all Bitcoin withdrawals were halted on Mt. Gox. In the wake of the Mt. Gox withdrawal freeze, the price of Bitcoin sharply dropped over 30 percent in February, but by the end of March, it was down over 50 percent. Users of Mt. Gox still maintained hope that the site would recover and go back to normal, but it was possibly the worst conceivable scenario that played out in the following weeks.

By August 2015, investigations led to gathering enough evidence to arrest Karpeles for fraud and embezzlement, and 650,000 BTC remained missing. Karpeles was only found guilty of fraud for manipulating the Mt. Gox accounting back end to hide corruption and/or insolvency due to stolen or misplaced funds. Close to the time of his arrest, a red daily candle marked the bottom of the Cycle 2 bear market, with a wick reaching as low as $162 and finally closing at $228 on August 17, 2015, representing an over 84 percent decline from top to bottom.

Figure 8

As the Mt. Gox scandal was in the process of unfolding, I was checking in with friends at work who were still actively involved with Bitcoin trading. I was clued in by the email communications coming from the exchange regarding the situation and discussed the possibilities of a recovery with friends who were locked out of funds. To this day, some people I know who lost money due to the Mt. Gox implosion never returned to invest in Bitcoin again. Watching Cycle 2 progress from the sidelines, I was grateful for the teachings of the community regarding securing Bitcoin and the use of the simple but effective mantra, "Not your keys, not your coins."

THE REBUILDING PHASE

In 2015, as the Bitcoin obituaries poured in over the course of the Cycle 2 bear market, my private keys remained secured in encrypted storage. Another coworker discussed giving up on Bitcoin, proclaiming that it was dead to him, and he showed me a new exchange called Coinbase, which I pulled up on my work PC. I gazed at the price on the simple interface, fluctuating around $420 in mid-2014. I remember thinking that it was interesting how people were in such a negative mindset in the aftermath of the Silk Road and Mt. Gox situation, and yet the price was well above its Cycle 1 high of just over $30 at peak. It also seemed interesting that new exchanges were being well funded, proposing to fix the problems of security and stability that plagued the Bitcoin space in these early years.

The sentiment from the perspective of most people I talked to at the time was very depressing, and the uncertainty around regulation in the United States was also starting to become an issue for potential investors, many of whom were now concerned with the IRS and how complex their taxes would be that year. Interestingly, the crash after the highs didn't deter true believers in the space, and new companies rose from the ashes of the bear market during this time. The process of recovery was underway for crypto, but it was also a time of recovery for me personally.

MOVING TO THE OTHER SIDE OF THE WORLD

Starting with my breakup in 2012. I had already been rebuilding a new life as a single adult, which was awkward at first but resulted in a mindset shift that laid the foundation for an adventure that followed. I was now a lead engineer overseeing a team responsible for the company's graphics engine that was used by each game studio. By this time, I was with the company for about five years working with an in-house OS, which was Linux based. Our graphics engine was a component of the OS, and so we had close relationships with the OS team as well as the game studio teams. Our most recent graphics platform was becoming more mature and stable over time, but earlier versions caused a bumpy transition leaving some scars on game studio engineers and high-level managers who felt like there was a case for an off-the-shelf solution.

Eventually, after some internal debate, our team attempted to defend the pros of a proprietary system, but the company decided that we would switch to an Embedded Windows and Unity-based platform to leverage off-the-shelf game engine tools for games going forward, so I tried to go along with this for some time in good faith. During the next few months, it was apparent that the Linux-based system would be phased out. We went from a tight-knit proprietary shop developing custom components to being reduced to more of a systems integration team beholden to the feature set provided by Unity's game engine, and the major shift from Linux to Windows.

Before long, many of our Linux experts resigned and the remaining team pressed on for a while, but the entire work environment had changed. This shift at work and in my personal life led to a moment of opportunity to make a significant change. My debts were all paid off, my graduate degree in software was complete, I was single for the first time in eight years, my company was transitioning from our custom Linux engine to an off-the-shelf Windows Embedded solution, and crypto was in a bear market. Adding to the storm of changes was a message from my landlord saying that the apartment I lived in was sold to another company and my lease would not be renewed.

In the final months of working for WMS Gaming (which was now Scientific Games), I took a vacation to go visit my youngest sister in Korea, and this is where I got the idea to quit work, get a teaching certificate, and move to Asia. The process was not simple, but after working through the CELTA program and interviewing for jobs abroad, I landed a one-on-one business teaching job at a place called Language Cube in Seoul, Korea. I sold or trashed all but two bags worth of belongings, my Bitcoin, and one guitar. In August 2014, I flew from Chicago to Seoul and found my employer-provided apartment where I'd stay for the next eight months.

ETHER ORIGINS

In mid-2014 while I was focused on getting my work visa and getting on a plane to move to Korea, another major event in crypto went under my radar: the early foundational development of the Ethereum blockchain. Vitalik Buterin, a co-founder of *Bitcoin Magazine* in 2011 in his late-teenage years, developed a passion for Bitcoin and became an expert in its technology stack. Absorbed in blockchain research, Buterin became interested in extending the functionality of Bitcoin, but the community rejected the idea of adding complications to the Bitcoin protocol, which would trade off security and stability for more complexity. The ethos of decentralization, stability, and security is the salient function of Bitcoin among many of its advocates, and Buterin thought that blockchain technology could do much more with some enhancements.

In November 2013, Buterin released a new white paper titled, "Ethereum: A Next-Generation Smart Contract and Decentralized Application Platform," which sparked a new discussion around the possibilities of having applications executing on-chain, meaning cryptographically secured so that in theory, no central authority could manipulate the rules baked into the programs running on the system. Ethereum allowed new "tokens" to be created with only a few lines of code, but it also allowed these tokens to adhere to "smart contracts," which would allow the creator to program a specific set of rules into the token's functionality, thereby making it possible to execute a software-based contract between multiple parties as an arbiter or automated escrow service without the need to trust a human to enforce the rules. Considering how expensive it is to enforce a traditional contract with each party involved potentially requiring legal services, the idea of smart contracts is compelling given that the cost of a few lines of code executing on the Ethereum blockchain is nowhere near what the typical legal firm charges per hour. On July 30, 2015, the Ethereum blockchain successfully launched and would soon change the cryptocurrency landscape significantly in Cycle 3.

TRILEMMA WOES

While Ethereum was getting off the ground, there was another important topic being discussed in the community leading into Cycle 3, and that was the need for scalability. The **blockchain trilemma** refers to the trade-offs between three aspects of decentralized money: decentralization, security, and scalability. The Bitcoin block size is limited to 1 MB and only one block is added to the blockchain every ten minutes, which meant that the number of transactions being processed and verified could not compete with modern payment systems, such as the major credit card companies.

At the time, it was thought that if Bitcoin was going to be digital peer-to-peer cash, it would need to compete with these already adopted mainstream PoS systems. The growing popularity of Bitcoin exposed this scalability and transaction speed problem when many new users flooded the **mempool** with pending transactions, which led to higher transaction fees as well as long wait times to complete confirmations. Innovators at this point had a few years to gain expertise in blockchain technology by absorbing the open-source Bitcoin technology stack and were plotting new solutions to these problems that emerged as the scale of new simultaneous users increased during Cycle 2.

CHAPTER 6

CYCLE 3

FORKS, ICOS, AND CASH COINS

At the end of the summer in 2014, I was invited to an event in Seoul for expats, or "foreigners" as they are usually called there. It was a long weekend in Korea for a holiday called Chuseok, when many of the local city dwellers travel to their parents' houses to gather and celebrate, leaving Seoul feeling like a ghost town. This event was unlike anything I had ever attended. It started at a bar called Sin Bin in the foreigner-friendly district of Itaewon. The foreigners all gathered on the rooftop of the building and a few people gave talks, almost like standup comedy but with a little bit of lecturing mixed in.

As a new foreigner in town, there were always new lessons to be learned from people who had experience teaching English in Korea. It was during this event where I met my future wife, sitting at the bar with a friend, and curiously not with family for the holidays. It turned out her parents lived in Malaysia, and this was a bar she had been an employee of in the past.

We exchanged phone numbers and soon developed a serious relationship rather quickly. This was completely unexpected, as I had no intentions of trying to start a relationship abroad, but I went with what felt right at the time.

This period for me was consumed by growing accustomed to a new language, new cultural norms, and new areas that were interesting to explore. I was quickly absorbed by the challenging work schedule, where I'd teach a wide range of lessons to students of diverse ages and levels of English proficiency. The work was challenging and rewarding at the same time, given that most of the lessons involved conversations with people from many different walks of life, primarily those who lived in the Gangnam district, best known as the luxurious setting where Psy filmed his popular music video for the hit song "Gangnam Style." I had signed a one-year contract, but it was cut short when I could not figure out how to satisfy management. It seemed like the new manager there wanted to find any possible reason to threaten me with termination.

In the first six months I was there, every week came with a new threat and, eventually, write-ups saying that I wasn't following school policies. This, I was told, is a very common practice of intimidation that is supposed to motivate new employees. Against the recommendations of friends and coworkers, I decided to put in the contractual two-month notice to resign and leave the country four months earlier than expected.

In April 2015, it was time to go back to the United States. I decided I would move to Portland, Oregon because of its better weather, growing technology hub, and an insanely great lineup of breweries. When I got back to Chicago, I bought a 2014 Chevy Volt, but it was newly titled, so I could get the federal electric vehicle (EV) tax credit of $7,500. Then it was a matter of packing all my things in the car and driving out west. With about $20,000 in savings and a small set of possessions that all fit in one car, I made it to Portland where a friend of a friend had an extra room in his house waiting for me in the Kerns neighborhood for $500 a month.

In Portland, I was still talking to my future wife over the phone almost every day, and her plan all along was to get a student visa to study cooking in Australia. I convinced her to come live with me and go to school in Portland instead. This meant that I needed to get financially stable and find a decent living space.

A few months before she arrived, I found a contract job with a company called Immersive Media in Washougal, Washington, just across the Columbia River from Portland, where I made iOS and Android VR video streaming apps. The first app was for NBCUniversal's launch of *The Expanse*, featuring spaceships that could be previewed in VR using a smartphone and the **Google Cardboard headset.** The not-so-pleasant part was the imminent drop-dead due date for Comic-Con that year where they planned to hand out Google Cardboard units at the NBCUniversal booth and promote their new TV series. With two weeks of dedicated programming, only taking breaks to eat and sleep, the app was a success at the convention. Immersive Media liked my work enough to offer me a full-time role as a dedicated app developer (both Android and iOS), and so the work continued with apps for various companies, including a collaboration with the *New York Times* developing nytvr, another project with a hard deadline due to being launched with a Sunday *NYT* edition that would include a new Google Cardboard headset.

Being the only developer for both the iOS and Android apps was intense, and I spent very little time doing anything besides coding and working with the *NYT* teams to meet their requirements before launch. The entire process was about two months of nonstop work, and I nearly quit the job afterward to find something else but was convinced to stay and continue different projects with a little more help and a more reasonable schedule.

It was right around this time that my soon-to-be wife relocated to Portland and started school. We decided to look for a house and I had saved just enough money for a 5 percent down payment with a budget of $300,000. But after three attempts at offers above the asking price and being outbid for the third time in a row, we decided to take a break from the house hunt and continued to rent for a while.

My company needed to hire a few more employees when we landed the contract to live stream the 2016 Olympic Games in Rio de Janeiro in 360 VR format. I was lucky enough to have some friends who worked with me at WMS in Chicago agree to move out and join me in Portland. We hired several more engineers for QA and web development for a browser-based front end. The company also added computer vision scientists to the roster since we were developing the camera systems from scratch. I ended up working mostly on the Toshiba camera module driver software that captured individual video frames from eight modules and the graphics pipeline that decoded the raw images and stitched it all together in a VR format.

By the time the Olympics were over, we had a well-put-together team and had overcome some serious challenges to get the live system working just in time for the games in Rio. The company was acquired by Digital Domain 3.0, and we were the VR arm of the company after that with me as the director of software engineering, managing a team of fifteen alongside our hardware team of about the same size. The fast pace in the growth of the company was indicative of the technology hype cycle that commonly resurges in various forms. I can already see a growing hype wave in artificial intelligence in 2023, as NVIDIA and many other tech companies capitalize on the narrative of never-before-seen innovations that will change the world at an exponential pace.

As 2016 came to a close, I was catching up on YouTube to have a laugh at the state of the ongoing election between Donald Trump and Hillary Clinton when something new came into my feed. The algorithm must have picked up on my Mt. Gox and other crypto-related emails, and Andreas Antonopoulos was the speaker in a new series of interesting lectures that I couldn't resist watching. I learned about his book *Mastering Bitcoin*, which I later read and thoroughly enjoyed. Another video suggestion looked interesting, so I continued down the new rabbit hole, where I eventually stumbled upon a lecture given by Amanda B. Johnson in her series *Dash Detailed*, which discussed the problems with usability in Bitcoin and how Dash aimed to solve those problems.

Dash is a portmanteau that combines the words "digital" and "cash," but what I didn't know yet at the time was that Dash used to be called Dark Coin when its privacy layer was the main purpose of creating the new cryptocurrency. Of course, long before this, my coworker had already mentioned this altcoin years ago at the WMS offices in Chicago, but back in 2014, I wasn't interested enough to go diving into the details. This time, I was hooked on learning all the new things evolving in the crypto space, and Dash captured my attention in a big way with its numerous innovations, including masternodes, treasury and governance, privacy, and instant transactions.

MASTERNODES

Dash's core software architecture is based on Bitcoin Core but includes a second layer of nodes called masternodes. A masternode is a specialized full node that provides extra services to the users of the base layer. To ensure that the second layer consisting of masternodes is incentivized properly without nefarious intentions, the masternode must post 1,000 Dash as collateral, which proves that the node has skin in the game. This collateral stays in the user's wallet and so the private keys are never relinquished to a counterparty. In return for providing useful services to the overall network, a masternode address is awarded 45 percent of the mining block reward when it is its turn in the queue of all active masternodes. Forty-five percent goes to miners who secure the network with proof of work, and 10 percent goes to a treasury that funds upvoted proposals that meet the minimum number of positive votes.

TREASURY AND GOVERNANCE

When a block is discovered using proof-of-work mining, 10 percent of the award is kept in a treasury. The masternode network votes on proposals that are on-chain requiring a proposal fee. If a proposal gets enough votes, the treasury funds the proposal with a monthly superblock disbursement, which is a fancy way of saying the blockchain automatically sends the proposed amount of needed funding to the public address that requested it. The incentives are aligned so that masternodes who own 1,000 Dash are motivated to upvote the proposals that most benefit the network. This governance model is what the community calls a DAO or decentralized autonomous organization.

PRIVACY

One of the masternode services is called Private Send. Dash has historically been lumped into the digital asset category called "privacy coins" because of the Private Send feature that provides coin mixing functionality among the second-layer masternodes. Coin mixing is also something that can be used to privatize Bitcoin transactions, but it typically gets done on a third-party service, introducing counterparty risk. Dash, on the other hand, does its mixing on the incentivized layer-two masternode network.

INSTANT TRANSACTIONS

Another feature provided by the masternode network is Instant Send, which can verify transactions within a subsecond time frame, allowing Dash to compete with existing mainstream payment technologies, such as credit cards when it comes to transaction settlement speed. The block time for normal transactions not using Instant Send is two minutes, so a typical Dash transaction is usually much faster than a transaction on Bitcoin's network. Due to the higher frequency and larger block size, a Dash transaction is designed to have very low fees in comparison to Bitcoin. The goal of competing with major credit card companies is to charge a fee lower than the typical merchant fee for each credit card transaction and be able to do it at similar volumes that can accommodate the bandwidth needed to keep up with worldwide commerce.

MY FIRST ALTCOIN TRADE

I was very impressed by these innovations and, before long, was convinced that this would be my first altcoin investment. Lucky for us, our house hunting was a failure, and the down payment savings account became my crypto fund for the Donald Trump era. Thanks to some extra cash coming in from the federal government for the purchase of my EV, I was able to scrounge up enough to invest in a masternode that I split down the middle with a family member. Bitcoin was starting to show signs of price appreciation throughout 2016, and before the year ended, it had rallied over $1,000 again.

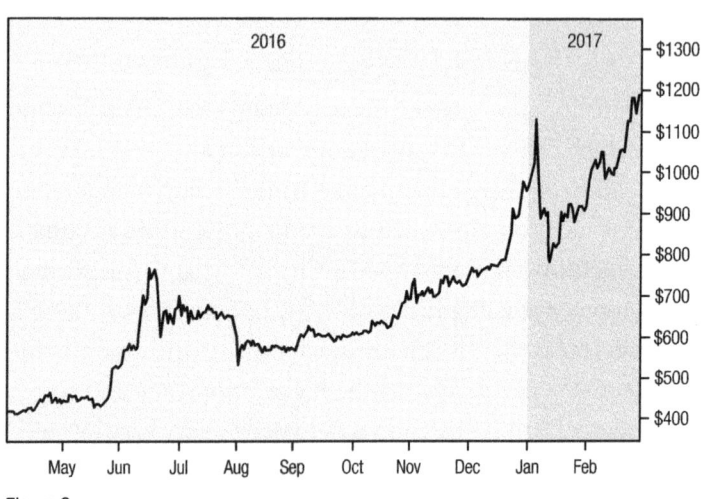

Figure 9

These were different times compared with today in the sense that altcoins were not readily available on popular exchanges such as Coinbase yet, and a typical altcoin pair on an exchange was only available for trade against Bitcoin in most cases. The platform I chose for my Dash purchases was Poloniex, but first, I needed Bitcoin to send to Poloniex before I'd be able to acquire Dash.

For the first time in years, I decrypted the vault that held my wallet.dat file from 2011 and downloaded the latest Bitcoin

Core client to get access to my stash. Unfortunately, there were errors syncing the blockchain and processing the old file. I saw the balance and the short list of transactions, including the beef jerky purchase and the send to Mt. Gox, but when I tried to send the remaining balance to Poloniex, a cryptic error occurred and I had to try resyncing the blockchain every time to try something different. This process of resyncing the chain was taking a lot longer now than it did in 2011, and so I gave up after a few tries. After thinking about it for a while, I did a search to figure out whether I could get my private key and somehow gain access to the coins another way. It turned out that a newer wallet app at the time called Electrum had such a feature called "sweeping" the coins from an existing private key. I looked up how to extract the private key that matched the public address with the non-zero balance to the command line in the core wallet, and sure enough, it worked like a charm.

Sweeping the private key in Electrum made the balance available to spend, and I was in business. After wiping my forehead over that drama, I also made a Coinbase account and went through the KYC/AML process. Unfortunately, my 3.6 BTC was not enough for a masternode, and I would need to wait what felt like forever to get approval to use Coinbase for fiat transactions. Eventually, I was able to buy enough Bitcoin to trade for a masternode, sending the BTC to Poloniex, making the trades to Dash, and then sending the Dash from Poloniex to the Dash Core wallet software on a laptop. When all was said and done, the masternode was purchased for a grand total of around $17,000, or $17 per Dash to get the full 1,000 DASH required for collateral. My half of the node was funded with some of the original BTC I had plus about $6,000 in cash.

The process of setting up a masternode was the next step, so I started looking around for help on the forums and came across guides that included using a service called Vultr to host virtual Linux instances which could run the Dash masternode software. Setting up a virtual machine was simple with Vultr and cost about $10/month, and the masternode payment schedule was roughly 1.8 Dash per week, or close to $120/month at the time, so it was well worth it. The process took a couple of hours including a step where the node running on the virtual machine (VM) must sync the entire Dash blockchain. Then there's a handshake transaction that must execute from the core wallet with the collateral address having exactly 1,000 Dash. Eventually, the success code appears on both ends and the status indicates that the masternode is in the payment queue. If the node is executing properly, the payments roll in, appearing as mining rewards. It was like printing money. This idea of staking a crypto asset and earning yield over time would eventually play out in fantastically complex ways in other crypto projects.

Dash was one of the first to develop the idea of a DAO as well as a staking system that still allows the owner of the masternode to keep their private keys safe. Later iterations of staking services that require users to send assets to a wallet hosted by the service do not achieve this important security feature.

Very soon after I set up the masternode, I was traveling for my company doing a sales trip in Israel when Donald Trump was inaugurated in January 2017 as president of the United States. During the trip, I also had an app tracking the Dash masternode value, which climbed from $17,000 to $118,000 after a presentation by Amanda B. Johnson at an event called Anarchapulco. It was as if the audience at these events was accumulating massive amounts of Dash while Amanda went through detailed presentations explaining the necessary evolution of cryptocurrency and how Dash could solve the problems of scalability and transaction speed to compete with the major credit card companies.

During the trip, I was thinking about Dash and its standing as a competitor to Bitcoin. To me and many others at the time, it seemed like altcoins such as Dash would overtake Bitcoin as the main peer-to-peer cash system. It was my belief that if a cryptocurrency could manage to succeed in providing a scalable solution that was cheaper than the existing credit card system, it made sense that the game theory would play out in such a way that the world would wake up to a new, more cost-effective system used for payments technology and adopt it to take advantage of the benefits.

I was reminded of the story of Steve Jobs and Apple going up against IBM. The dominant company and legacy computer industry were taken over when a wave of innovation that Apple brought to the industry revolutionized the PC and the common person was able to wield the power of digital computing. In a similar way, Dash was paving the path for the average business accepting traditional forms of payment to cut out the existing payments middleware, reducing merchant fees, and this was a value proposition that I was in support of given that the consumer is burdened with the overhead costs of these legacy systems that are so entrenched in our economy.

MINING IN CYCLE 3

As Cycle 3 progressed, I was working with some friends to research mining again and came across Bitmain's products. ASIC miners were necessary to contribute any meaningful hash rate for Bitcoin mining, but Dash's X11 hashing was still being done mostly on GPUs. A company called PinIdea was making a Dash-compatible X11 ASIC, and I placed an order for one DR3 X11 miner at a price of 0.72 BTC plus 0.03 BTC for shipping. The invoice was dated January 7, 2017, at which point 0.72 BTC was the equivalent of $650 with Bitcoin trading at under $1,000.

Hi there. Your recent order on PinIdea - Mining Device for DASH and More has been completed. Your order details are shown below for your reference:

Order #269

Product	Quantity	Price
ASIC X11 Miner DR3	1	฿ 0.72000000
Subtotal:		฿ 0.72000000
Shipping:		฿ 0.03264257 via Flat Rate
Payment Method:		CoinPayments.net
Total:		฿ 0.75264257

Figure 10

The miner arrived and I collaborated with a coworker to set it up in Washington where the energy bill would be a bit cheaper. We fired it up and set up an account with a mining pool where we were immediately at the top of the hash rate contribution list, competing exclusively with GPU miners. This led to a very quick recovery of the price of the DR3 as we also watched the Dash price appreciate. As more Dash-compatible ASIC miners came online, which happened rather quickly, our slice of the hash rate pie dwindled, but unexpectedly, aftermarket prices for the DR3 skyrocketed as PinIdea could not keep up with production of the DR3 to satisfy an explosion in demand.

This led to another idea: selling miners for profit in the aftermarket. PinIdea's orders were backed up, and after some emails with their support channels, it became apparent that they would be an unreliable supplier, but Bitmain had a more mature operation since they had been in business a while longer, having produced the top miners for Bitcoin. Then they started making miners for altcoins such as Litecoin and eventually Dash. The Litecoin miner was called the L3, and I was able to purchase five units in an early batch. As I waited for the miners to arrive, the prices of all cryptocurrency assets were climbing, following Bitcoin's lead. This caused a demand frenzy over miners, and a friend hooked me up with an entrepreneur who was building out a large mining operation in Washington. He was paying us $5,000 per L3 miner, which was roughly a 230 percent markup, or a profit of $3,500 per unit.

Rather than attempt to start our own mining operation, this seemed like a simpler business with a lot less risk, leveraging our relationship with Bitmain to be early in the queue of customers buying miners and selling them in an aftermarket frenzy while asset prices appreciated. By this time, Dash had already reached over $200 per unit, and Coinbase was beginning to add new assets to its exchange. Having sold all miners as they arrived, by the end of the cycle I was relieved when I noticed that all the miners plummeted in value, and many became unprofitable to run in the worst of times for altcoin prices.

I was especially relieved that we never pulled the trigger on building out our own mining operation. We were considering buying laundromats, which had the electrical capacity built in for the dryers that we could plug miners into. There was also a facility near the Columbia River that we almost rented, but the HVAC buildout would have been too costly with a far-out break-even date, so we backed out of the deal. There were close calls along the way that could have played out terribly. I knew some aftermarket sellers who waited too long in the queue to get D3s with the intention of selling them in the aftermarket and watched their value plummet from thousands down to under $100 as mining with those machines became unprofitable.

THE COINBASE EFFECT

The first new asset to show up on Coinbase after Bitcoin was Ether (ETH), the token used on the Ethereum blockchain. Ether is used to execute smart contract code, which incurs fees called **gas**. The more code the GPU miners must execute to process a smart contract, the more gas was paid in ETH in the transaction, and gas fees are also higher when there is more demand for transactions on the network.

I was generating good income with mining and masternode operations, so I saw this as an opportunity to diversify some of those earnings into Ether. I picked up 20 ETH on January 8, 2017, at just over $10 per ETH. The Coinbase effect, as it is now called, was a phenomenon related to the popularity of Coinbase and the difficulty to use fiat currency to buy altcoins. Shortly after listing on Coinbase, an altcoin's value would rise sharply. Ether had a few factors at the time that caused the price to soar quickly: (1) It wasn't very well known yet by all market participants what Ethereum was; (2) It was listed on Coinbase in late 2016, which was before Cycle 3 really picked up the pace; and (3) Ether was starting to be used to create many new tokens in what are called initial coin offerings (ICOs). An ICO allows an individual or group to create a new token sale to raise capital for a project without having to go through traditional investment means, such as venture capital or public offering of shares through an IPO. These ICOs ramped up in popularity, creating many new crypto tokens and caused massive waves of speculation over new projects. Many of these were pump-and-dump cash grabs, but the key to Ethereum's rise to be the number two cryptocurrency behind Bitcoin was that all these ICOs used Ether as the gas to execute contracts on the blockchain, and to do this meant having to purchase Ether. A record of my first Ether purchase in Coinbase shows how fast I went from an initial investment of $210 in Ether on January 8 to taking profits of over $7,000 only five months later. Ether's price had climbed from $11 to over $417, a rise of 3,680 percent, or close to 38x.

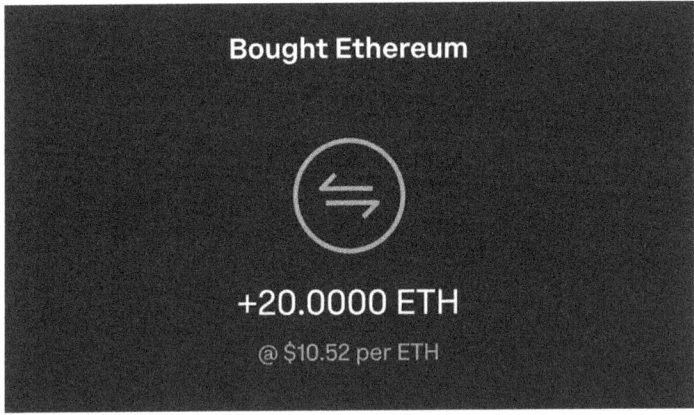

Figure 11

My gain at exit was close to a 35x return, which at the time was a difficult exit to make because in these moments, I found myself at a crossroads. What if the price could go much higher? Would that really happen given it was already up 38x? How does one even process this rapid growth, especially facing a potentially life-changing moment? Seven thousand dollars was a lot of money to me at the time, and I also had to contend with the idea of losing it if the price crashed as Bitcoin did in 2011. How would I feel then if I watched thousands of dollars in gains disappear?

When a potential profit is gained that I would not want to lose, I tend to take some off the table or put in stop-loss orders that automatically sell the asset if prices are falling below a threshold. If my initial risk is low and I can stand to watch and wait as things progress, it is easier to hold a position, but it never ends up being simple because a long-term thesis tends to be at odds with trading for profits. For example, with Dash, it seemed obvious to me that it should overtake Bitcoin as the number one crypto asset, which created a conflicted mindset. I hadn't thought of an exit strategy for Dash, which is often a recommended thing to do when investing in any asset. Why would I sell if I believed this new technology was the next big thing? These early convictions that inspire an investment can cause an irrational loyalty, especially when getting involved in the project directly through forums, voting in a DAO, staking in a smart contract, or other agreements that can cause friction when there is a good opportunity to sell. I've also found that it's helpful to take losses if a thesis didn't work out as expected and reset mentally. Every new trade can be thought of as a clean-slate scenario so that it doesn't come with the baggage from previous trades that put unnecessary pressure on the next decision.

THE BITCOIN CASH HARD FORK

While I became absorbed in the community of Dashers, voting with my masternode for proposals and maintaining my Vultr masternode instance, there was another similar conversation heating up online over transaction speed and scalability in Bitcoin. The Dash developers made their own version of a digital asset that could solve the problems of peer-to-peer digital cash, but other interested parties wanted the Bitcoin network to adopt changes that would enhance scalability so that Bitcoin could evolve to compete with the existing centralized payment rails. To do this, Bitcoin would have to increase transaction bandwidth, and one proposed way of doing this was to increase the block size to accommodate more transactions per block.

A proponent of this proposal, Roger Ver, was an enormous influence on Bitcoin. He was nicknamed Bitcoin Jesus for his evangelism and investments in the nascent digital asset class in the early days, and he even owned the domain name bitcoin.com, but when Ver started to advocate for controversial changes to the Bitcoin network, it led to a holy war between original Bitcoiners and the supporters of changes to make Bitcoin more like a scalable cash system. A group formed to support the changes in the Bitcoin network and decided that they would fork the Bitcoin blockchain to preserve their accounts and transactions on the ledger up to a certain block height and, from there, create support of the new chain with new rules so that miners would decide which chain was the real Bitcoin. This "hard fork" resulted in a debate over which blockchain was the real Bitcoin, but the new chain was given the new name Bitcoin Cash (BCH). An interesting effect leading up to the fork was a massive migration of capital from altcoins back into Bitcoin due to the known date of the fork giving people the opportunity to stack up as much BTC as possible and then receive an equal amount of BCH at the Bitcoin address on the day of the fork.

I didn't make any moves in this lead-up to the fork because I had a Dash masternode in the layer-two payment queue and was earning a nice steady yield that I would lose if I made any trades. In fact, my thought process at the time led me to see the Bitcoin situation as a big mess that I wanted to stay out of, and Dash was proving to be a far better project given its governance system. It allowed the Dash network to make decisions, such as block size increases via the voting process on-chain, rather than duking it out on Reddit in a social media battle royale.

The whole ordeal led me to have more conviction that Dash was potentially going to overtake Bitcoin as the main cryptocurrency, and so my decision was to stay in Dash and stay out of Bitcoin for the time being while the fork wars escalated. This was a time of uncertainty for the crypto markets. Dash, after posting an all-time high of $240, quickly fell to a low of $115 in seven days and then recovered to $200 only four days later. These swings represented ridiculous volatility in my portfolio given that it moved 1,000x the price of Dash with a masternode.

To put this in perspective, every time Dash moved by $1, it created a $1,000 swing in the masternode's value. On a typical day, the price could swing about $10–$50, representing moves of $10,000–$50,000 in my portfolio. I somehow got used to this and managed to suspend any fears over this radical volatility. Initially, it was outlandish to think that these swings in value were greater than my entire net worth only months prior. I lost sleep on certain days, and it became a common practice to wake up to my alarm, grab my phone, and look at my portfolio value before even turning the alarm off. Usually, it was a matter of seeing how Asia was reacting to the news. Looking back on it, I feel like this type of behavior was completely unnecessary given that I didn't plan on selling anything that day. Somehow, the psychology of money causes people to become obsessed and irrational.

The Bitcoin Cash fork successfully launched on August 1, 2017, causing market volatility as liquidity then suddenly poured out of Bitcoin and back into altcoins. Now that the first block was mined on the BCH fork, those Bitcoin addresses also held an equal balance of BCH. I remember some critics positing that this was like fiat monetary debasement in the way that it represented a printing of free money like how central banks increase the monetary supply. Some Bitcoiners undoubtedly took advantage of the fork by selling BCH directly for BTC, growing their stack, while some people who believed in the BCH chain being the real Bitcoin likely did the opposite, selling all BTC for BCH. Another group looked at this as an airdrop or dividend and sold the BCH right away for dollars. Whichever camp the owners of Bitcoin found themselves in, the fork initially caused a lot of uncertainty.

When prices stabilized, BCH became the number three cryptocurrency in September 2017 behind ETH in terms of market cap while Dash also remained in the top ten but lower on the list. The entire cryptocurrency market cap at the time was nearly $170 billion, of which Bitcoin itself was valued at nearly $75 billion. Dash's price went over $400 per Dash, and then another major price correction to the downside followed. After a bit of a lull period, the market recovered, but the Dash price trickled downward to $270 over the course of about a month, when in November the real euphoric move started for all cryptocurrencies.

EVERYONE'S A GENIUS

The end of 2017 was a period I like to call the "everyone's a genius" phase in the crypto space. There wasn't a single project that didn't seem like the best innovation in money, and many soothsayers on YouTube appeared with technical analysis, price predictions, investment advice, and the typical tribal commentary over which projects were better than others. ICOs were popping off left and right with outlandish valuations in massive price pumps as traders attempted to grab cash out of the market. By the end of November, the Dash price reached over $800, making the masternode worth more than $800,000. Now I had some serious thinking to do. With every masternode payment yielding over $1,000 worth of Dash every eight days, it was very difficult to imagine selling the collateral now and losing that income. There was also no sign of the market slowing down as the mainstream news was picking up on the price action.

Speculative commentators gave wild price predictions at the time, claiming that Bitcoin could surpass $20,000 per Bitcoin. These numbers seemed completely unrealistic a year prior when Bitcoin was still under $1,000, but the word about crypto was spreading during the holiday season, and just before Christmas, Bitcoin finally reached its cycle peak at $19,891.99 on Coinbase. Dash, in a single day on December 20, swung between a low of $1,050 to a high of over $1,600 and finally closed at $1,524 that day marking the cycle top. The masternode had gained almost $500,000 in value in a single day!

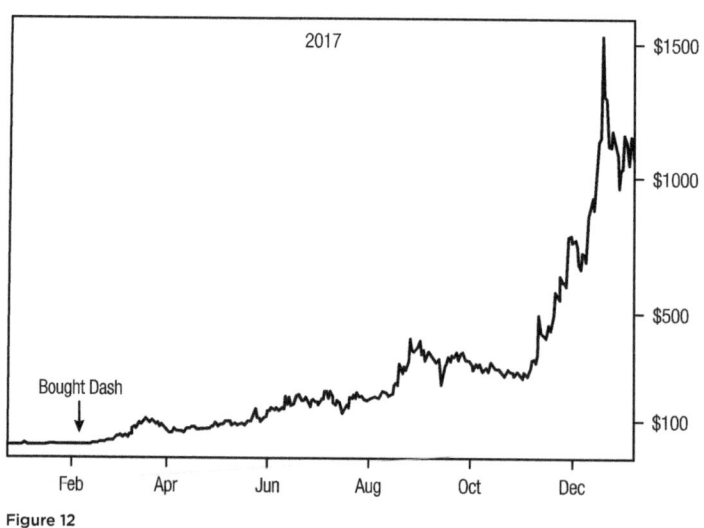

Figure 12

A realization came over me when researching tax laws, and since I didn't own the masternode for over a year yet, it meant taking short-term capital gains if I sold before February. Additionally, I was enjoying generous masternode payments each week and selling newly minted Dash at these elevated prices.

So again, I decided to hold on and continue the ride, but it was only a few days of volatile downside that ripped Dash back down to a price under $1,000, eventually settling in near $1,100 but with wild and puke-inducing volatility.

I was watching my net worth swing hundreds of thousands of dollars per day and still basking in a euphoric haze wondering how high things could go. Not many people seemed to think prices could crash at the time because we were in the new paradigm phase of the bubble cycle. A friend from high school was in town and we went out for some brunch at Screen Door on Burnside and sat at the bar. The waitstaff and the busboy were all smiles and chatty about their crypto gains. They were recommending all kinds of coins they had purchased. I was getting calls from people I hadn't heard from in a while asking how to buy XRP and other altcoins.

My boss at work was now following the action as well, and he let me in on the old wives' tale of traders on Wall Street knowing when to sell as soon as the cab drivers in Manhattan are giving trading advice. Certainly, this was the frothiest time I remember in my experience with cryptocurrency. Everyone believed it would just keep going, even when the next price drop came. It was like the times before when the fear, uncertainty, and doubt (FUD) was flowing, and no one cared to listen to concerns or people who said it was an irrational bubble. Those bearish naysayers were idiots, and we were all going to the moon! Of course, we all believed the market would recover and all these prices were somehow justified, even though most of these projects weren't used much for any kind of real-world transactions outside of trading. There was real growth and adoption, but there were still major hurdles to overcome if Bitcoin or any other cryptocurrency was going to be accepted globally as a major financial asset, and we all just decided to basically ignore the facts because we were riding high on euphoria.

My time as a millionaire, at least on paper, was short lived. Soon after the eruption to all-time highs, a major price correction surprised a lot of people when Bitcoin Cash was suddenly added to Coinbase on December 19, 2017. The Coinbase effect kicked in and BCH rose to about $3,700 while BTC dropped to about $10,400. On some exchanges, the valuation of BCH versus BTC reached almost 0.4, meaning 40 percent of the market cap size of Bitcoin, the highest I've ever seen any other cryptocurrency come to be valued versus Bitcoin. There are still some believers in the **Flippening** with ETH being in the lead now as the number two cryptocurrency, but so far, Bitcoin has held the number one spot since the beginning when it was the first and only one.

Dash fell to under $800 in January, and as I waited for long-term capital gains to kick in, the bleeding continued. The day of Super Bowl LII, February 4, 2018, I don't even remember the game at all because I was too busy refreshing my portfolio on my phone, watching as the Dash price tumbled to under $500. This was the capitulation moment that got me serious about exiting before losing any more unrealized gains. I slowly started averaging out of the market, and there was a healthy bounce over $700 per Dash when Amanda B. Johnson was giving lectures at the Anarchapulco conference again. It was the back-to-normal phase that helped my cause, but when all was said and done, I calculated that about $1 million in unrealized profit was gone when including the brief all-time high of over $1,600. In other words, at the high, the $17,000 investment was at 94x the cost basis, but the realized gains ended up closer to 30x. Selling would prove to be the right move because the market didn't recover and carry on higher, but instead, the bubble kept on deflating and prices continued lower for several months through the bubble-popping phases, all the way down to despair. By the time Dash bottomed out, it was under $40 per Dash.

THE SEC TAKES ACTION

Around the time Bitcoin Cash and Bitcoin were fighting for liquidity on Coinbase, there was another catalyst that led to uncertainty in the Ethereum ecosystem sparked by the SEC, which took notice of the calamity in the cryptocurrency space. What I wasn't aware of at the time was that nearly all ICOs were infringing on securities laws. It suddenly became important to understand the regulatory frameworks of these financial assets from the perspective of governments. Experts at the time started to apply the **Howey test** to attempt to determine which cryptocurrency assets should be considered securities instead of assets.

Earlier in March 2014 after the Cycle 2 peak, the IRS published Notice 2014–21, which brought some clarity to the classification of Bitcoin from the point of view of taxation. This notice did not recognize Bitcoin as a currency but instead more like property like real estate "that has an equivalent value in real currency." The good news was that this meant Bitcoin was not regulated in the same way as a security but more like a commodity such as gold. As the cryptocurrency space evolved with Ethereum and other new projects, it became apparent that the IRS and the SEC would have to do a lot more to provide regulatory clarity for digital assets.

In 2018, the SEC cracked down on some projects for breaking securities laws when unregistered ICOs were determined to be pump-and-dump cash grabs. This became a very common formula that I've seen so many times over that it astonishes me to see it continue to work time and time again. Typically, the project claims to be an innovative, decentralized community or bank token, when in reality, it's typically based on a copy of some smart contract code for a token on Ethereum that issues most of the tokens to the founders. This initial distribution is called a **pre-mine** because even proof-of-work cryptocurrencies can be coded in such a way that the founders get an immediate chunk of the total supply at launch before any mining is done. The way these schemes usually transpire is with the founders marketing the tokens with celebrities and/or YouTube videos and then dumping their pre-mined tokens in the middle of a price pump. The SEC caught on to this and started cracking down heavily on such scams in 2018, which amplified uncertainty in general over whether some cryptocurrencies would end up being regulated as securities, further putting downward pressure on the market.

MASTERNODING

After taking healthy gains from the Dash masternode, I wasn't quite ready to give up on the market. A typical bear market starts with a big move to the downside and often takes waves of downside moves before bottoming, but after the market was down 50 percent or more, it seemed reasonable to believe that the worst was behind us. Of course, this was a mistake, but I generally only bet what I'm willing to lose on risky projects in crypto, and I went down the risk curve in 2018. Having large gains from Dash didn't help because it made bigger bets seem less risky.

A site called masternodes.online provided a list of cryptocurrencies that support masternodes, many of which simply copied Dash's code and model. Some of these projects started out yielding over 100 percent of the initial collateral investment year over year. This is how I learned a hard lesson about yield in crypto. A too-good-to-be-true yield is typically a sign of a honeypot that attracts new investors and most likely results in a pump-and-dump run on pre-mined coins that the creators gave themselves at the outset before any other participants could obtain coins. There is also a diminishing yield when new masternodes flood the network because the payment queue gets longer, causing the superblock pie to be diluted, and high yields have the effect of attracting more people to join in a race to the bottom.

Nevertheless, I got myself into a handful of these projects, getting masternodes started on Vultr for Innova (INN), GoByte (GBX), Bulwark (BWK), and Polis (POLIS). I planned to use all masternode payments to buy and stack Bitcoin, and initially, this worked out somewhat well until yields started to drop along with the asset prices as the bear market progressed to the despair stage. I gave up on the operation and was able to liquidate most of the collateral by exchanging it for Bitcoin except for Bulwark, which eventually died off after a litany of 51 percent attacks, forks, and service disruptions. This was the first time I watched an asset I owned go to zero, proving that it's possible to lose everything somewhat easily in a crypto investment. The silver lining was that I only bet what I was willing to lose on these projects, which was a small percentage of total 2018 gains, and I had some Bitcoin rewards to show for it that I kept in cold storage. This experience was a painful yet important one that helped me reframe my understanding of yield in crypto, and this would be useful knowledge in Cycle 4.

THE VR BUBBLE

Being into cryptocurrencies during the 2017 bull run was exciting and lucrative, but it only served as a decent distraction from my real-world problems. After being promoted to direct the software team at Digital Domain, the VR space became flooded with competition, and it was becoming clear that the market demand for 360 video technology was not going to support all the various products being produced by a litany of new startups and major tech players alike. We were having some success building out the tech, but in the end, sales and revenue weren't sufficient to justify the operation. The VR hype cycle seemed to be coming to an end and our office started laying off most of our staff. I was tasked with letting go of most of our team and keeping part of the team until a specified date so that we could finish an SDK product, after which I would also be let go with severance. The promise of VR and the marketing blitz failed to capture a profitable return on investment, so I took a new job in a much different industry at a company called moovel where I found a role as an iOS developer for public transit applications. Eventually, crypto came back on my radar because Bitcoin's price dipped again in late 2018 to around $3,000, and Dash was back to under $100. I joined a three-way split on a Dash masternode, and I picked up a third of the collateral at a cost basis of just under $50 per Dash. I also set up an automated dollar cost average (DCA) schedule with Coinbase for Bitcoin.

Figure 13

By January 2020, I had already moved to the Bay Area in California for a job at Apple that started in November 2019. After getting some cheap crypto in the bear market and kicking off the new year with a new gig in Silicon Valley, I was getting optimistic about the future. What happened next was quite unexpected.

CHAPTER 7

CYCLE 4

INSTITUTIONS, DEFI, AND "STABLE" COINS

In early 2020 with my automated periodic DCA strategy, a new Dash masternode generating crypto income and my new job as a software engineering manager at Apple, I was once again happily distracted from thinking about my investments for a bit and more focused on ramping up my contributions in my new role. My wife had traveled back to Malaysia to see her parents, but I stayed at our new rental in San Jose to focus on work and tried to settle in a bit more. On the second leg of my wife's trip while in Korea, the news broke out about a new virus originating in Wuhan, China that was likely to cause travel shutdowns, so she was lucky to get out of Asia just before Korea grounded flights and shut down travel in and out of the country.

I had a bachelor party to go to in Los Angeles, and after returning home, I was extremely ill for a few weeks. It's possible that this was the first variant of SARS-CoV2, the cause of COVID-19, but there wasn't any convenient way to test for it at the time. Shortly after this in late February 2020, my grandmother passed away in the suburbs of Chicago. I went out to visit, noticing that travelers were more often wearing masks, and airports were oddly empty. I started to get more curious about the novel virus, but it wasn't considered to be a major threat in the United States yet. While I was in Chicago, I met with some old friends and remember the shoulder-to-shoulder crowding in some places, where nobody seemed worried at all about yelling in each other's faces over the loud music, and there was not a single mask to be seen in the crowd. This was the last time I would be traveling for a while because in March, a state of emergency was announced, starting with cases of the virus increasing in New York and eventually making an appearance in Santa Clara County, where I lived, with twenty known cases on March 6. It was at this time Apple announced that all employees in Santa Clara were encouraged to work from home if they were capable of doing so. I was able to pack up my things at the office and move my setup to a spare bedroom that would become my home office for the next two years.

    The prevailing rumor at the time was that it would take two weeks to "slow the spread," which was woefully inaccurate. Case numbers began to balloon everywhere throughout the United States and in other countries where the virus was already penetrating deeply into the population for which it was proven to be deadly, especially for aging demographics in places like Italy. Then the government stepped in and initiated lockdowns, and it quickly became apparent that the economy would absorb a massive negative impact from the radical policy shifts. The unemployment rate spiked as companies shut down operations, and the stock market along with crypto quickly tanked. In the three weeks from February 24 to March 9, Bitcoin went from around $10,000 to a low of under $4,000, losing over 60 percent of its valuation.

In the investment community, the coronavirus is what is called a **black swan event** because of its unexpected nature and detrimental effect on the economy and markets. Even though this presented an incredible buying opportunity at unexpected lows, it simply wasn't a priority for me to make plays in the market at the time. The news surrounding the pandemic and what it meant for our future was mainly what captured my attention, aside from keeping it together at work and staying on target with the projects I was responsible for.

In terms of financial strategy, it was more of a deer-in-headlights feeling of being frozen without knowing what to do besides hold on and hope that this was only temporary. This is when I started getting more interested in understanding the responsibilities of the Federal Reserve because what they did next was an unprecedented expansion of the money supply to avoid an economic crisis. Put another way, the economy was falling apart and the Federal Reserve had a solution: print money until the printer runs out of ink. Of course, there's no ink involved because it's only numbers in a computer system, but the money supply suddenly jumped 20 percent, and the markets quickly recovered their black swan losses.

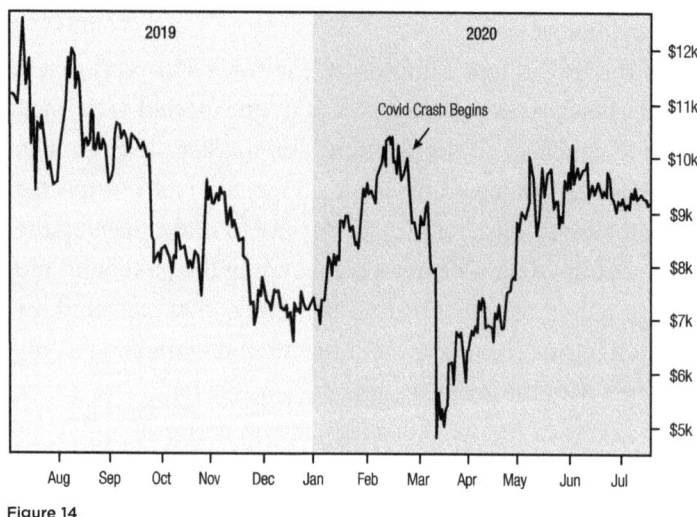

Figure 14

Ever since the GFC in 2009, the Federal Reserve uses a tactic called quantitative easing (QE), which is a technical term used for buying assets, and interest rates can be decreased, enabling the Fed to create looser economic conditions for banks in hopes that liquidity will trickle into the economy at large and stave off recessions. When interest rates are low, businesses and other debtors are getting cheaper money when they take out loans from banks. The low rates incentivize spending this new money created out of thin air, and this provides a boost to economic activity. It also ensures that the government can take on more debt at low interest rates for economic recovery programs and stimulus checks, which were issued to encourage consumer spending. When it became apparent that lockdowns would continue based on case numbers and hospitalizations increased without enough medical knowledge to treat the nascent viral disease, it led to the government providing these programs as a countermeasure for shutting down businesses and eliminating jobs.

When new money entered the system, it chased after goods and services, increasing demand, while the supply side suffered from the effects of safety regulations that resulted in shutdowns of production facilities in many areas throughout the world. Another knock-on effect of extra liquidity in markets occurs when excess capital that wants to find a destination ends up invested in assets, and this results in stocks, real estate, and cryptocurrencies all absorbing the extra liquidity. I saw this emergency capital injection playing out in late 2020 after the US presidential election in November, and this is when I decided to go all in on crypto again.

GOING ALL IN

The general election in the United States in 2020 was an entertaining spectacle of populism and heated debate, but I had something else to worry about at the time because Bitcoin was responding to Federal Reserve policy changes, and not all my cash was readily available to invest. I thought about the time back in 2011 when I considered selling my 401(k) to buy Bitcoin at $2 but didn't pull the trigger and asked myself if I'd miss out on all the potential gains again. After some contemplation, a strategy formed. The first step was to accumulate the remaining Dash needed for a masternode to run on my own again, and then I'd need to move some funds around to go all in besides enough to cover the bills plus a month or two buffer. I sold some old mutual funds I went into right out of college and liquidated a Roth IRA account as well. Then I also made the calls to withdraw my 401(k) accounts from other previous employers. I rolled most of the 401(k)s into an IRA and took out $50,000 in cash after allocating some for taxes with the 10 percent penalty. With all the new liquid cash I'd be able to buy more Bitcoin, and I also decided to acquire an Ethereum 2.0 validator node. The Ethereum 2.0 project was the anticipated **proof of stake** network update that allows a node to lock up 32 ETH and earn compensation for staking on a validation instance running the Ethereum software. Luckily, I wouldn't have to run the software components myself because of a service called allnodes.com, which manages the node for a fee and lets the user keep the private keys. I used the same service for Dash, so all payments were sent directly to cold storage, but for Ethereum 2.0, there was a catch. The smart contract for the proof of stake validation node required locking the 32 ETH and leaving the compensation locked in the contract until the new system would eventually go live. I knew this was a risk, but it seemed like a manageable risk to take given the Ethereum 2.0 launch would take place as planned. When I started accumulating with the goal of getting 32 Ether, 1 ETH was $546. The Dash node was a greater risk in terms of invested capital, and my cost basis for the collateral of 1,000 Dash ended up around $80,000.

My overall hypothesis was that this was only eight months or so after the halving in March, and if things worked out as they did in the previous cycle, there should be plenty of upside left to go through 2021 into the holiday season, which is consistent with the four-year cycles of the past. The estimate at the time for the Ethereum 2.0 main network launch was only about one year away at the time, so it didn't seem like too much of a risk to lock up a node for a year and be able to sell it in 2021. Most of my remaining cash went into Bitcoin, and even in my IRA, when the funds became available, I went in on GBTC, the Grayscale Bitcoin Trust shares. I had around 80–90 percent of my net worth in crypto assets at the end of 2020 when Bitcoin was nearing its previous all-time high, bumping up on resistance of $20,000. I was confident that it would all work out on

New Year's Eve after finalizing all purchases. It seemed like a perfectly reasonable thing for me to be almost all in on crypto, without much doubt at all.

My YouTube feed was full of bullishness, and there was a lot of speculation over the early development of decentralized finance (DeFi) which primarily used Ethereum smart contracts. The government was printing stimulus checks, and the speculative machine kicked into high gear when assets of all kinds started rising in US dollar-denominated value. When Bitcoin broke $20,000, it pumped massively, going higher than $24,000 in a few days. We were off to the races in Cycle 4. The break of all-time highs brought on an explosion of media attention, a beacon signal to new investors who were waiting on government stimulus checks to land in their bank accounts. After a short consolidation period of around five days, the wind picked up in the digital asset sails again, and day after day Bitcoin floated as if it were on a magic carpet made of government cotton used to print dollar bills all the way up to $34,000. Ether also pumped to $1,000.

Dash, which had been my lead horse in the race in 2017, wasn't performing as expected and was hindered by an announcement that it would be removed from an exchange due to concerns over privacy features and regulatory issues. This seemed a bit nonsensical considering Dash remained on plenty of exchanges including Coinbase but nevertheless created a scare early on in Cycle 4 about the future of private transaction regulation and hindered price action for privacy coins when the rest of the market was going wild.

It's hard to predict what will happen with altcoins in an environment where there isn't regulatory clarity. It took a few days for Dash to rally, and it swung wildly up to over $150, back to $100 a day later, and then settled in around $130 for a bit before dropping right back to $100. I wasn't sure what to make of this, but something was off. First, I was watching too closely for this not to affect my emotional state. With the 1,000x multiplier, the roller coaster was nearly vomit inducing. I still thought that Dash would beat the all-time high of over $1,600 later in the year, so I brushed it off and continued holding.

Bitcoin continued upward to over $40,000 before entering one of its standard volatile corrections of over 30 percent, which didn't seem to scare the veterans at all, but newcomers who showed up in droves amid news of the all-time highs found themselves riding the roller coaster that not all participants end up surviving. There were price predictions of over $100,000, even $300,000 coming in for the end of the year on popular YouTube channels, and the inevitable endless waterfall of speculation on Twitter. It was like no one could lose because the Fed was pumping the market, and everyone had nothing to do but stay locked up in their houses watching the charts and Bitcoin YouTube while waiting for another **stimmy check** from Uncle Sam so it could be dumped into the markets with the expectation of producing easy gains.

INSTITUTIONAL CAPITAL

In late 2020, a company I had never heard of called MicroStrategy was on the Bitcoin YouTube scene with the CEO, Michael Saylor, giving interviews on many YouTube channels as well as CNBC. Saylor was exploring ways of preserving wealth as the US dollar expansion caused currency debasement. Although the rate of inflation is often measured by the prices of goods and services, the currency supply also tends to grow with banks creating new loans and governments providing stimulus checks. This currency debasement form of inflation is thought to be like an invisible tax on holders of money already in existence, and some analysts including Saylor calculated the rate of debasement to be around 15 percent per year on average. If this is the case, it means that cash sitting in the bank loses 15 percent of its value in a year, and after four years have passed, it will be valued at 52 percent of its original purchasing power, assuming the same rates of debasement continue each year.

A corporation like MicroStrategy that has cash on its balance sheet must eat this loss of purchasing power, and if the company wants to hold value for the very long term, it's a risk that should be weighed with other options. Gold is also mined at around 2 percent stock per year and has a high stock-to-flow ratio, but Saylor argues that it's not clear how to know the amount of gold in existence or whether new gold could be discovered, changing its supply dynamics. For Saylor, the only institutional investable asset in existence that provides a predictable outlook on supply and sits outside of the traditional financial system is Bitcoin. This is only a basic description of the thesis that Michael Saylor presents in many interviews. For a more comprehensive understanding of the philosophy behind MicroStrategy's investment in Bitcoin, I recommend the Michael Saylor series on the *"What Is Money?" Show* podcast hosted by Robert Breedlove. Saylor put his company's money where his mouth was and started accumulating Bitcoin using the cash on MicroStrategy's balance sheet. On August 11, 2020, MicroStrategy acquired 21,454 BTC at an aggregate purchase price of $250 million. Saylor continued to make appearances on mainstream news and podcasts and still into late 2022 hasn't sold a single Satoshi.

In early 2021 as Bitcoin's price neared the $40,000 level, MicroStrategy held a webinar where various panels discussed how corporations could benefit from this new investment opportunity. Then it was on Twitter where things became even more interesting when Elon Musk and Michael Saylor had a brief exchange in public. Elon asked if large transactions were possible on the Bitcoin network, and Saylor was quick to point out that not only is it possible, but he would be happy to share his playbook with Musk.

On January 29, 2021, Elon Musk changed his Twitter bio to the Bitcoin logo, and the market erupted, sending Bitcoin from $30,000 back to over $38,000. Days later on February 8, a press release headline from CNBC read, "Tesla buys $1.5 billion in Bitcoin, plans to accept it as payment." In a single day, the price pumped from $38,000 to $46,700. By February 28, Bitcoin put in a new all-time high of $58,385. This rally lifted Bitcoin's market cap above the $1 trillion mark and set off a wave of euphoria and speculation in altcoins.

The markets had begun to froth up like they did in 2017 with many new projects gaining attention. With increased ad budgets, companies and services promoted new methods of earning yield on cryptocurrency. The promise of high yields for staking assets in DeFi and centralized finance (CeFi) produced a wave of new companies and financial services in the cryptocurrency space. With new companies and funding popping up to capitalize on the hype, there is always an influx of **Ponzi schemes** and nefarious actors in the space attempting to capture the excess liquidity for themselves.

THE DEFI AND CEFI HONEYPOT

Earning yield (or interest) on cryptocurrency became a hot topic of discussion at the outset of Cycle 4, and it was something that came on my radar when the founders of a new company called BlockFi entered the space. The business model allowed customers to send assets to the centralized service and earn interest in **stablecoins** which are pegged to the US dollar. BlockFi also offers loans that can be taken out in stablecoins to be paid back with interest, and the loan is also usually backed by collateral that a customer sends to the service to back the loan. This process of borrowing and lending on a centralized service is called CeFi because custody of the assets is managed by a centralized counterparty. DeFi is a relatively new innovation that utilizes smart contracts and DAOs to execute the rules of a borrowing and lending system on a blockchain such as Ethereum.

When I invested in Ether in late 2020, it was because I knew that these innovations would drive up transaction volume on the Ethereum network, causing transaction prices to rise and therefore should cause price appreciation in the asset required to execute these contracts as demand went up. In December 2020 when I was accumulating Ether, there was a little over $20 billion locked up in DeFi smart contracts. By February 2021, there was over $50 billion in DeFi contracts. The price of Ether was strongly correlated with DeFi TVL (total value locked), which rose to $2,000 per ETH in February 2021. The yield for staking crypto assets often significantly exceeded the interest paid by traditional banks in savings accounts, creating an attractive option for new investors.

I wasn't interested in getting into CeFi because I never like to trust another party with my coins. The lessons of the past made it clear that holding the private keys to a cryptocurrency asset is necessary, or else the purpose of the technology is defeated. This didn't stop many others from dumping their assets into the DeFi and CeFi systems, and I must assume many were compounding leverage to bet even further on the progression of the bull market cycle. In this leverage scenario, an investor can buy an asset such as Ether, then take out a loan against the collateral, which can then be used to buy yet more Ether or other crypto assets, and the chain continues so that an initial investment is compounded with debt. The problem with this leverage chain is that the cryptocurrency space is volatile, so margin calls were frequent in market corrections and unwinding would occur quickly and violently to the downside in these chain reactions. This liquidation of assets became a common event in Cycle 4, and with other derivative instruments being played by institutions, it only caused more complexity in the price action.

The raucousness in price action led to a much different market structure throughout 2021, and it was beginning to become hard to navigate. This led me to take profits somewhat early on to ensure that I wasn't still over 80 percent into risky assets. I cut down my position by about half, including breaking up the Dash masternode, and rebalanced more into Bitcoin, which seemed like a safer play going forward. However, I did take some risk with the gains and purchased some meme coins that would eventually make Cycle 4 much more interesting.

THE RISE OF DOGE

During the **Everything Bubble** that frothed up in the massively debt-leveraged economy, memes on Twitter, especially the ones showing up on Elon Musk's account, became a significant factor in creating multibillion-dollar waves of capital to rush into Dogecoin. In early February 2021, Musk tweeted, "fate *loves* irony" and added that an outcome where Dogecoin became the currency of earth would arguably be the most entertaining and ironic. These statements came shortly before Mark Cuban, owner of the Dallas Mavericks, announced that his NBA team would accept DOGE for tickets and apparel.

Dogecoin is a blockchain asset with a code base forked

from Bitcoin, with a couple of important modifications that were meant to poke fun at blockchain technology. For one thing, Dogecoin has no max supply limit and can be mined indefinitely with new block rewards adding to the total supply. Second, the current total supply is over 100 billion DOGE at the time of writing, which leads to a phenomenon called **unit bias**, or a false comparison of price per unit when considering an investment. People often buy a so-called cheap coin rather than Bitcoin because they think it has more potential to rise in price, and they think owning more units matters. What really matters is the underlying value of the asset (the market cap), but human psychology can often be irrational.

At the time Musk first tweeted his "fate *loves* irony" message with all crypto Twitter watching, Dogecoin was priced at $0.007 per DOGE, or less than a penny each. Shortly after the tweet storm that started a new wave of popularity for Dogecoin, it was announced that Musk would be the host of *Saturday Night Live* (*SNL*). Rumors began to circulate over whether Musk would talk about Dogecoin during the NBC appearance. I decided to make a small side bet on another dog coin that appeared on the Ethereum blockchain called Akita Inu (AKITA). There were some new meme coins like Akita Inu and Shiba Inu at the time with enormously high supplies. Akita Inu's max supply is 100 trillion tokens, and the price was a small fraction of a penny. I wanted to be a billionaire AKITA holder and only needed $150 to get there. On May 8, 2021, an audience of 7.3 million tuned in to watch Musk on *SNL*, and the price of 1 DOGE went up to 45 cents, a gain of over 6,000 percent since Musk's first tweet. I hadn't looked at it in a while, so I opened my wallet to look at my AKITA stash and my $150 had turned into $50,000, a 330x gain! I quickly ran for my Trezor, plugged in, and connected to Metamask to swap the tokens for USDC stablecoins to lock in the profits. This turned out to be a **buy the rumor, sell the news** event, and the top was in during the live airing of *SNL*, followed by a DOGE decline back to 16 cents in a few days. Because I was curious about the rise of AKITA and SHIB, I found out that both coins were added to Poloniex (the same exchange where I bought my first Dash in 2016) and rocketed upward in price shortly after the listing but especially during the Elon Musk *SNL* episode. The craze over "dog coins" continued, and many more Inu tokens were created on Ethereum, some of which also gained popularity. This wild investing atmosphere was becoming overheated, but in the euphoric stages of the bubble, the new paradigm mindset takes over, and no fundamentals need apply.

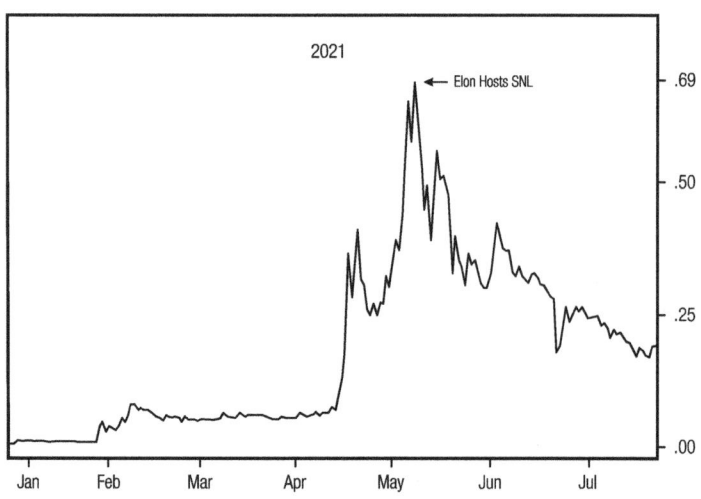

Figure 15

NON-FUNGIBLE TOKENS

A non-fungible token (NFT), unlike Bitcoin, is not fungible by design, meaning that it's meant to be unique. An easy example to illustrate the utility of an NFT is tickets to see a show at a theater. Each token represents a seat in the theater, and patrons purchase tickets in the form of an NFT, which reserves one unique seat per token. In this way, the ticket vendor doesn't have to worry about a double spend or whether the ticket is swapped or sold. This mechanism offers another form of digital scarcity whereby an individual item can be referenced. Therefore, it's possible to designate an item as the first of its kind or even the only one. Consider the value of an art piece that is the only one of its kind. The most expensive art piece ever sold up until today is a painting called *Salvator Mundi* by Leonardo da Vinci on November 15, 2017 for $450,300,000. The most expensive NFT ever sold until now is called Everydays: The First 5000 Days by Beeple on March 11, 2021 for $69,300,000. My first encounter with NFTs was in 2018 when I discovered CryptoKitties, a series of NFT cartoonlike cats, with an additional feature in the smart contract code that allows owners to breed cats with different features to create new kitties in the family tree. There are many more uses for NFTs aimed at pinning anything that is not fungible to a token. For example, there are companies like SolidBlock that are offering real estate tokenization.

An NFT can include added features that determine the terms of a contract. For example, the original artist can include a royalty rule that transfers a percentage of the sale price back to the originator, without the need to involve lawyers or brokers. Another rule for real estate could be to allow many owners who don't even know each other to own shares of a property and receive proportional rent payments through blockchain smart contracts. Of course, the metaverse is also a place where digital real estate has started to utilize the NFT standards on various blockchains.

Celebrities who own land in the metaverse can attract new nearby landowners who are willing to pay high rates for the luxury of living next to their favorite celebs' digital worlds. In virtual worlds, there are already large economies for virtual goods. The value proposition for NFTs elicits controversy among varying people and industry moguls, but regardless of individual opinions, there is a frenzied market that is hard to ignore.

During the 2021 Bitcoin bull run, cryptocurrency once again gained the spotlight in mainstream culture, and NFTs started showing up everywhere. I didn't plan on buying any NFTs at the time, but a YouTuber and comedian named Brent Pella did a charity NFT sale and his lineup of NFTs was reasonably priced, so I picked one up. It was a two-part video series NFT called *Spirit Airlines Animated Stand-Up Comedy*. Maybe someday if Pella is hosting the Oscars, these should be worth a lot more than what I paid, especially if he gets slapped in the face live on the show.

ALT SEASON

There are multiple definitions of **alt season** (sometimes #ALTSZN on social media), but the colloquial gist of what defines an alt season is Bitcoin's price going sideways after a euphoric bull market phase and altcoins exploding regardless of fundamentals. The term "**pumpamentals**" is used to describe a coin's ability to pump, such that it deserves to be joined with other speculative coins in one's altcoin bags before the impending alt season.

The hallmark of an alt season period is Bitcoin dominance sharply moving downward as the altcoin total market cap explodes to the upside. In Cycles 1 and 2, there were not that many altcoins, and so the alt season phenomenon arguably applies to only Cycles 3 and 4. In 2018, the alt season period was the height of irrational exuberance and marked the beginning of the end for the bull market, followed by a gradual decline into the bear market, and the end of April 2021 was no different.

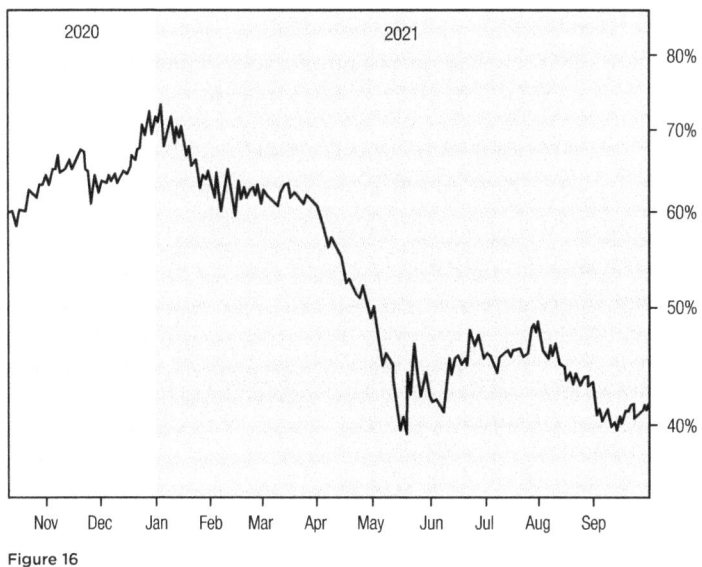

Figure 16

Between April 1 and May 18, 2021, Bitcoin dominance fell from over 60 percent down to just under 40 percent. Bitcoin's price during this time was going sideways in the $50,000–$60,000 range. Ether, which tends to lead other altcoins, climbed to an all-time high of $4,384 by May 12, 2021, and many other altcoins manically jumped to new all-time highs as well.

Dash, which had underperformed the entirety of the bull market, didn't get close to an all-time high and topped at $476 in Cycle 4, still over a 5x increase from late-2020 prices. I was more aware of the urgency of the situation this time than I was in 2017, and equipped with experience, I was able to force myself to go against euphoria and took some profits on Ether and Dash throughout 2021. However, it was confusing because Bitcoin dominance under 40 percent and alt season seemed to show up too early. It was supposed to happen in November or December based on the four-year cycle theory.

The altcoin party ended abruptly when China announced that Bitcoin mining was officially banned, ironically something a lot of Bitcoin advocates were hoping would happen. A major concern growing in the Bitcoin community was an authoritarian government like China's gaining the ability to attempt 51 percent attacks on Bitcoin's blockchain. By banning mining, China only further decentralized the mining network as the companies in the region relocated to various mining-friendly zones throughout the world. But in peak irrational form, the market was spooked, and Bitcoin's price dropped to $50,000. This didn't seem like an issue at first that would be a risk to the bull market cycle as the Federal Reserve was still spiking the punch bowl, and Bitcoin's price was still near $50,000, which only seemed like a typical correction, just like those seen in 2017 on the way to the blow-off top.

THE ELON EFFECT

A day or two later, Elon Musk announced via Twitter that Tesla would no longer accept Bitcoin as payment, citing climate concerns as the reason. Again, this pushed the market into a free fall, and by May 19, Bitcoin's price slammed down into the $30,000 level, where it finally bounced more than halfway down from its new all-time high. When the dump started, I sold half my Dash to secure profits. This type of reactionary trading is hard to resist in moments like these when thousands of unrealized gains are melting away in minutes. I will admit that I'm not immune to panic selling, especially if I'm watching profits disappear at such rates. The Bitcoin market is still small enough that it reacts quickly and ferociously without any breaks. The market doesn't close like the New York Stock Exchange and rages on 24/7. In a precarious situation like this, it can be better to scale back risk just to be able to sleep at night rather than stay up late, glued to price action, and managing orders.

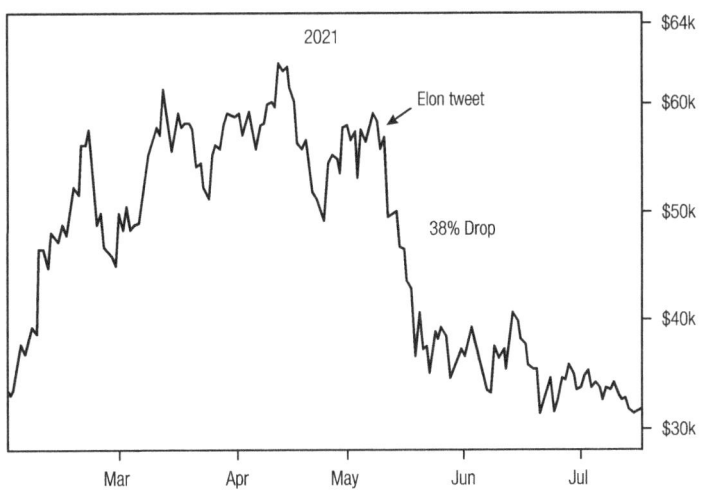

Figure 17

According to the mainstream, Bitcoin was dead (again), and alt season was apparently over. There was a brief period just before Musk's tweet where it was thought that this could be a typical bull market correction. Most predictions that followed the four-year cycle theory, based on the Bitcoin halving cycles, were focused on the end of the year being the topping-out phase of the bull run. Most commentators seemed to think there would be another blow-off top as seen in all previous cycles, whereas in 2021, there was no such thing, only a choppy distribution pattern of ups and downs ranging between $50,000 and $60,000. This led to some interesting speculation over why this time was different, and for me, it seemed like a good time to cut any losses or take whatever gains were left, and continue to hold my long-term position in Bitcoin.

It seemed to me that a 50 percent correction was not like the typical 30–40 percent corrections seen in previous cycles, so I didn't want to get caught up in hope again like how it worked out in 2018 on the way down. This is where I started to learn to go against my emotional tendency to hold on and hope for a recovery, as many others did. There were many YouTubers still proclaiming that the bull run wasn't over, but I didn't care to find out with all the risk still on the table, so I exited my Dash position fully and rebalanced again. For me, being risk averse was having a modest position in Bitcoin and some still in Ethereum given that my validator node with 32 ETH was still locked up in the Ethereum 2.0 smart contract. I went from being close to all in to being carefully positioned in the span of half a year.

THIS TIME IS DIFFERENT

The ranging and distribution pattern at the top of Cycle 4 in early 2021 felt a lot different than the exponential incline of 2017. After the initial climb to almost $60,000, Bitcoin's price ranged and formed a longer choppy top pattern. The $60,000 level seemed to be a strong resistance, and because it got there so quickly in 2021, it wasn't matching the time frames predicted to be the duration of the full cycle. This may have been the leading factor in keeping people in the market, hoping for that next wave above $60,000, but it didn't come. Instead, the rising wedge pattern played out as probability suggests it should, which is to the downside. There was a strong bearish sentiment when Bitcoin's price capitulated at $30,000, and social media was back to work with arguments over where the bottom would be. In these cases, I've found that many contributors to the conversation rely on historical data to predict future outcomes. This is always the case even though the digital assets market is evolving rapidly, and the **macroeconomic environment** is also changing over time.

At twelve years of age, Bitcoin had a fair bit of history behind it, but I have some arguments that suggest history is not a good indicator of future outcomes when it comes to crypto and Bitcoin. First, twelve years seems like a long time for Bitcoin, but it is not a long time in the big picture, and given the 2009 launch when markets were close to bottoming in the GFC, this represents a time of lows where upside potential would have been close to a maximum. There has not been a deep recession since due to loose monetary and fiscal policy from 2009 up until 2022. Now that the Federal Reserve began tightening financial conditions and raising interest rates in 2022, we've seen yield curves invert, which is typically an early sign of a deep recession on the horizon. Time will tell if this plays out, but it's important to be aware that no recessions show up between 2009 and 2022 aside from the COVID-19 crisis, which was quickly ameliorated with an unprecedented inflationary monetary policy to avoid economic collapse. The second argument is that the market has evolved drastically since Cycle 1. Cycles 1 and 2 did not include many altcoins, and Ethereum with all its ICOs and honeypot DeFi tokens did not exist yet. Arguably, Cycle 3 was the last retail-dominant cycle, which could explain its price action following a more predictable psychological pattern that matches the classic bubble, with a new paradigm style blow-off top.

Cycle 4, however, proved to be tricky with what seemed to be layers of strategies and distribution cycles mixed in with retail influences. The big players showed up in Cycle 4, such as Elon Musk and Michael Saylor but also hedge funds with their sophisticated trading models and tools. When most of the liquidity in the market is driven by "smart money," the expectations must change. There are plenty of tricks and games that these big players have up their sleeves, and the average retail trader doesn't have a chance against this experienced edifice of institutional capital. I started to think more deeply about this and concluded that I was early to the party in 2011, but that didn't mean I could compete and trade the same way I did in the past in this new environment. Short-term trades were not a practiced skillset for me, and Cycle 4 proved this to be the case. Another thing I realized in Cycle 4 was that "cash coins" such as Dash were no longer nearly as relevant as they were in Cycle 3, which led to another general lesson to be wary of expecting past innovations to be valued in the future.

There could be any number of changes in the sentiment of the market by the time there is a new mania phase, and it would take hours of research to form a thesis to predict which trends will be hot down the road. I appreciate spending time to learn new things and grow with the space, but the more lessons I learn, it seems the more I recognize that a modest position in Bitcoin is all I really need to be in the game and stay interested enough in the space to continue learning more. I remain dedicated to the thesis that I always want to have some Bitcoin as insurance against a bailout-driven economy, averaging in when the despair stage kicks in.

LENGTHENING CYCLE THEORY

With each new cycle, new theories emerge as well as YouTubers and analysts who promote them. I had been following along with a new theory called lengthening cycle theory, which looks at previous bull market cycles and determines a start and an end date to calculate a duration. It turns out that Cycles 1 and 2 are shorter in duration from bottom to top than Cycle 3, and Cycle 1 is shorter than Cycle 2 when duration is measured from bottom to top.

The fact that there was no blow-off top yet in Cycle 4 and that prices were recovering in late 2021 suggested that this theory could play out, and a blow-off top might not arrive until later in 2022 or early 2023 based on the expansion rate of previous cycles. The price was ranging from $30,000 in May 2021, up to $69,000 in November, and back down to $33,000 before bouncing upward again. Because $33,000 was a higher low than $30,000 and $69,000 was a higher high, the market remained somewhat bullish in the hopes for a new leg upward.

At around $35,000 per Bitcoin, I decided to place a big bet on Bitcoin with my 2021 profits in late January 2022. Bitcoin's price started ranging upward again, driving further bullishness in the market and lending credence to the lengthening cycle idea. There are a couple of problems with this lengthening cycle theory. For one, the first cycle is probably not great data to include since it didn't start with a halving or any major influx of capital. The market was too small to compare this cycle to any other. This only leaves two cycles remaining as historical data points, which means that it could only go in a binary direction. Either Cycle 2 is longer than Cycle 3 or vice versa, and Cycle 3 just so happened to be longer than Cycle 2, but this is not enough data to suggest a trend that plays out many times over.

There is another issue with focusing only on a few historical data points, which is that it completely ignores changes in the macroeconomic environment. Russia invaded Ukraine and provoked the European Union and United States to apply economic sanctions on Russia in February 2022, and the Federal Reserve announced that it would be hiking interest rates after the **Consumer Price Index** (CPI) started to poke its ugly head above 5 percent in late 2021. The Fed also announced that it would start quantitative tightening (QT), or the opposite of easing.

Although Bitcoin formed an upward channel, reaching $48,000 by late March 2022, the headwinds of the macroeconomy and a shift in global order created downward pressure on asset prices. All at once, the stock market and the cryptocurrency market seemed to correlate in lockstep and deflate like a balloon. I was aware of these conditions but didn't pull the sell trigger in time to take gains before it was too late. Only after Bitcoin neared my recent cost basis of $35,000 did I finally sell my big bet on a lengthening cycle at a small loss. The roller coaster was back to where it started. The lengthening cycle theory was busted, and the all-time high at $69,000 in November 2021 ended up being almost exactly at the same duration from the previous bottom to top of Cycle 3. Given that the market was now bearish, a cascade of deleveraging began, and what came next was even more spectacular of an implosion than I thought possible.

"STABLE" COINS

When I first discovered Tether, it was 2016 and I was making my first Dash purchase on Poloniex. I saw the ticker USDT at the very top of the list of unfamiliar altcoin assets and did some research on it. In 2014, the company iFinex Inc. in Hong

Kong created Tether Inc. which launched the project. iFinex also owns Bitfinex, one of the leading exchanges. The purpose of the project was to create a digital blockchain asset pegged to the US dollar, which provides the utility of trading in and out of digital assets quickly and being able to send a USD-valued token via blockchain rather than going through banks. Considering banks typically have a multiday waiting period for ACH transactions, this made trading in the digital asset space much more streamlined. The adoption rate proved its success, and from January 2017 to September 2018, the amount of USDT outstanding grew from about 10 million to about 2.8 billion, roughly equal to those figures in US dollars.

The value in USD is not always exactly equal to one dollar due to fluctuations in demand. For example, if the market experiences heavy volatility to the downside, people panic and run to safe havens, including Tether. In this case, owners of Tether can have sell orders above $1 that fill because the market isn't offering any at $1. Controversy arose when it was noticed that issuance of new Tether typically came shortly before Bitcoin price movements to the upside. This was suspected to be artificially adding liquidity to the order books and propping up the prices of assets. Because Tether Inc. did not reveal the portfolio of backing assets in its early days, it left people guessing if the company was actually solvent or created a sleight-of-hand operation with the ability to print free money, like a Ponzi scheme, if new participants continued to keep Tether tokens in the system.

In contrast, on July 22, 2022, there were over $150 billion worth of stablecoins out of a total cryptocurrency market cap of $1.043 trillion as reported by cryptomarketcap.com. This represents over a 53x increase in stablecoins from September 2018 in stablecoin value and a 14.3 percent slice of the total crypto pie. That percentage might go down if another bull market rally begins and stablecoins flood back into assets, but regardless, the growth of stablecoins is becoming a significant factor in the digital asset space. Tether inspired a trend, and new tokens in the stablecoin class arrived on the scene.

Stablecoins can come in a variety of types that have different characteristics. For example, USDC is a stablecoin by Circle that is also centrally managed like Tether. DAI is a blockchain-based MakerDAO-managed stablecoin. In contrast to centralized stablecoins, or DAO-managed stables, an algorithmic stablecoin is meant to remove the counterparty risk of a centralized counterparty or DAO management.

On April 24, 2019, Terraform Labs launched an algorithmic stablecoin system with a "burn and mint equilibrium" strategy that utilized the Terra (LUNA) token as an absorption mechanism for volatility, with TerraUSD (USDT) being the pegged asset to the value of the US dollar. The Terra blockchain also supported a borrowing and lending protocol called Anchor that returned a high yield of 19.45 percent on USDT tokens and paid the yield in LUNA. This yield was such an enticing honeypot that it drew in a massive amount of capital, totaling $18.64 billion by May 7, 2022. This date corresponds to Bitcoin's price falling off a cliff from $38,000 to $25,000, and because people were exiting positions so rapidly, all at once it created a run on Terra's bank.

There are also rumors of the Terra founders having involvement in the exit before the collapse, but regardless of who did the deed, it was an ugly cascade that followed. USDT lost its peg, which created a death spiral bank run, and to counteract it, LUNA was printed in massive quantities, debasing the backing asset in the process. LUNA reached an all-time high of $119.51, a market cap of over $40 billion in early April. By early May, only days after the USDT peg was lost, the token went completely bust losing nearly 100 percent of its value. The term "contagion" refers to knock-on effects from related systems causing even more damage in the process of a wipeout like the Terra decline. The Luna Foundation Guard (LFG) was a nonprofit entity that was originally set up to create a Bitcoin reserve to support the Terra blockchain and had amassed over 80,000 BTC in its reserves. When the USDT peg broke, this capital would have needed to be used to support the peg of USDT, but it's unclear what happened at this point. Bitcoin's price wavered near the $30,000 level for a few weeks before falling off another cliff, finally capitulating at a low of $17,500.

The contagion was far worse than a simple mashup of USDT, LUNA, and LFG Bitcoin reserves. Other borrowing and lending services started to fall like dominos, freezing accounts from gaining access to their assets, and in some cases declaring bankruptcy, or in more dramatic cases ended with founders disappearing and taking capital with them. As the details started to surface, it became clear that many of the people involved were taking on heavy risk behind the scenes and, in some cases, disappearing with investors' assets. It's sad to see people get hurt in situations like this, no matter how much responsibility lies on the investor in a risky market. Contagion is also a function of reputation, and like how Mt. Gox and Silk Road created a negative connotation surrounding Bitcoin at the end of Cycle 2, the Terra/LUNA/Anchor/3AC collapse is yet another reputational wound that will likely cause outrage pointed in the direction of the entire cryptocurrency space.

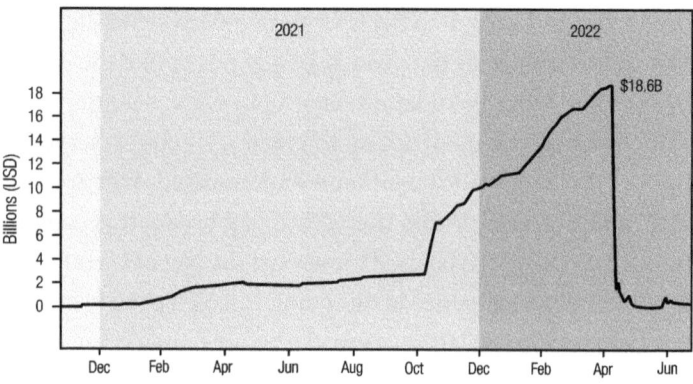

Figure 18

Interestingly, I discovered that this wasn't the first time in history that a system like Terra existed. It is well before Bitcoin's existence that pegged currencies have been implemented to solve the same problem of volatility in global markets. In 1997, the Thai baht was depegged from the US dollar and experienced a deep decline of around 60 percent of its USD value. Sometimes it fascinates me to uncover these historical events that suggest I've been under an illusion of safety. As a US citizen living in the States, it's easy to forget that the US dollar is nothing but a monetary tool, with no backing asset. It has become a belief system strongly embedded in our culture. If nothing we use as money is of intrinsic value, then what keeps the world believing in it? The number on the screen in our banking or investment account? The paper in our wallet and the government that issues it? Bitcoin's appreciation in dollar terms during recent years in which the US dollar was heavily debased has raised awareness of this illusion of stability, as sound money acts as a countermeasure to the common trap of fiat currency corruption.

PART III

LEARNING FROM THE PAST, SPECULATING ON THE FUTURE

CHAPTER 8

LESSONS LEARNED

BUBBLES AND FAIR VALUE

Acknowledging cycles in Bitcoin's price history is a way of clearly defining bull market mania phases and bear market despair phases along the arrow of time. The cycles can be thought of as ups and downs or peaks and troughs, but it is one thing to look at a price chart and a completely different scenario to have a large position and live through the intra-cycle price action. When participating in the mania phase of a cycle, which typically ends shortly after the top is in, there is clearly a recognizable feeling to it, and there are patterns in the charts that represent the market psychology as shown in the classic bubble chart.

What isn't obvious during the wild price swings is the consistent trend of adoption that can also be shown through blockchain metrics, such as the number of active wallet addresses, or addresses with a specified balance. This adoption trend is also apparent in the mining data. Total cumulative mining hash rate is one simple metric that has been in a consistent uptrend throughout the history of Bitcoin mining, partly due to the evolution of mining hardware but also because of the waves of new participants in the network. The adoption pattern for Bitcoin follows a curve that closely matches the adoption of the internet during an offset period. This curve is called a logarithmic regression, and if Bitcoin adoption were to follow the current trend, there would be close to a billion cryptocurrency users by 2025 compared with just over 100 million today.

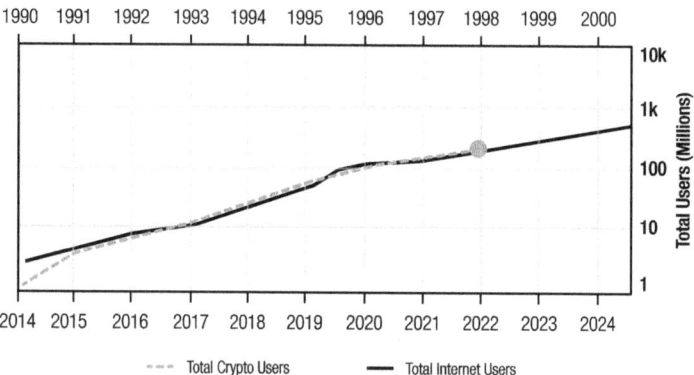

Figure 19

This trend occurs when a new technology is gaining adoption on what is called an "S-curve." S-curve adoption gets its name from the shape of the adoption pattern on a linear scale over time. It ramps up slowly at first before the technology matures and becomes more accessible, rockets upward when the majority flocks in, and then slows down with diminishing acceptance from the remaining laggards who fight the new technology until it is necessary to adopt it.

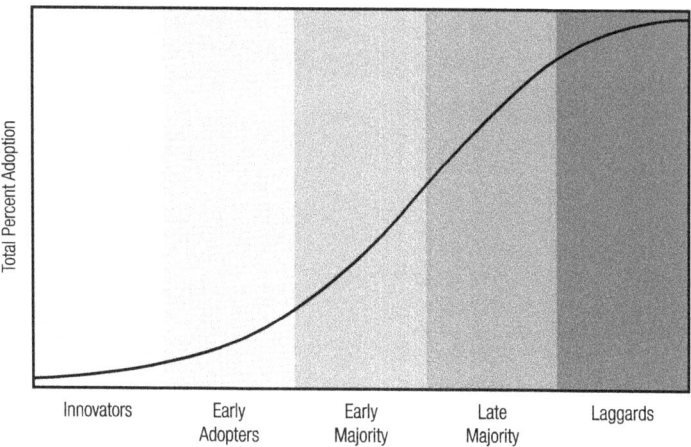

Figure 20

The Bitcoin price relies on many factors, such as the money supply growing with QE, but a significant factor aside from new money is Metcalfe's law because the network's value is determined by a function of the number of participant nodes in the system. Radical changes in monetary policy can have unexpected effects on price, but as adoption grows, the price per Bitcoin tends to trend upward over time, with the mania phases creating a superposition of bubble price added to fair value price. This can be represented by bands that track fair value and predict maximum bubble territory. A BitcoinTalk user named Trolololo originally shared this model in 2014.

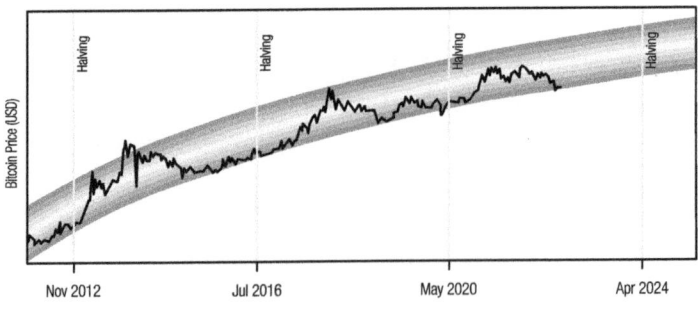

Figure 21

The rainbow is used to color code the bands where logarithmic regression determines the future price levels assuming Bitcoin stays on an S-curve in its adoption cycle. In its history, the price has always come back to the bottom band when it isn't overvalued, and the floor is determined by the network value, the mining cost per Bitcoin, and other factors.

Considering that the chart was developed in 2014, it's held up extremely well throughout the years. Buying while the price is in the blue band would have certainly paid off for anyone using the chart to determine entry points into the market, and selling in the upper bands would have also been a winning strategy for a swing trader. A historical trend of diminishing returns can also be gleaned from the chart by looking at the tops as they have been printed in lower bands with each cycle. This indicates diminishing volatility over time as the market absorbs more share of overall capital. The chart can't be a perfect predictor of the future, but it represents a mathematical adoption curve that has historically played out with other technologies that took time to be adopted and then developed into mainstream standards.

A common misconception of Bitcoin is that it's only a bubble and has no intrinsic value. Another way of wording this argument is that it's only speculative. I agree that Bitcoin does have a speculative component, and this speculative fervor drives massive swings to overvaluations, but the fair value as a function of adoption has remained steady on the S-curve. The unfortunate result of this combination is that the mania phases act as a beacon for new investors to arrive at the worst possible times, when prices are in overvalued territory, and the probability of ending up with short-term losses is high in these scenarios due to the speculative component significantly impacting valuation. This can be discouraging or even infuriating given that the drawdowns from highs are typically close to 80 percent. However, after making this mistake myself in Cycle 1, I've come to understand that there is more than mere speculation contributing to the value of Bitcoin, and it is still in an early stage of its S-curve adoption path. Assuming that the total addressable market (TAM) for Bitcoin is the 5 billion people who have access to the internet and half of those represent the serviceable obtainable market (SOM), using an estimated figure for the number of Bitcoin users at 150 million people, the current adoption rate would be 6 percent (out of 2.5 billion)—meaning another 94 percent of the SOM remains available to join the Bitcoin network as a new user. Even if the SOM were only 20 percent of the TAM in this case, it would be roughly 1 billion people, and the remaining SOM to join the Bitcoin network would be 85 percent. Since Metcalfe's law states that the value grows geometrically (not linearly) with the number of users, this does not mean an 85 percent gain in price. It would mean a 44x increase in value, or in dollar terms, an increase from $22,000 to $968,000 per Bitcoin. This dynamic of currently low adoption is why analysts use the phrase "asymmetrical upside potential" because a vast majority of the potential upside is untapped. These price valuations might also require consistent trends in Federal Reserve monetary policy. If a massive wave of deflation enters the markets and the dollar strengthens aggressively, future USD valuations would require updated calculations. There is a lot of uncertainty involved when calculating future prices of an asset, and times like these where the Federal Reserve is enacting a much different monetary policy using QT will most likely play a significant role in markets.

BITCOIN IS THE BOSS

Regardless of all the arguments for altcoins being a better investment than Bitcoin, the market cycles have always followed Bitcoin's lead, and Bitcoin's price movements tend to lead the altcoin market. It's debatable whether the halving is the most significant event that leads to a new bull market phase or whether Satoshi purposely aligned halvings close to presidential elections so that political populism would play a significant role in the cycles. So far, there are three distinct speculative bull market cycles that appear to be supercharged by the miners suddenly earning half as much Bitcoin with the same amount of mining power. This supply dynamic must have an impact on the market, but there are also many other factors in the macroeconomic environment to consider, such as central bank monetary policy and government fiscal policy. Because halvings have a way of landing in the middle of election years and populist politics tend to favor the perception of a strong economy, this leads to more monetary expansion to support generous fiscal policy. It may be pure coincidence, but there are some correlated data points to consider, such as times when the US government raised the debt ceiling and the correlation in the price action of Bitcoin and other digital assets.

US National Debt
(Trillions of USD)

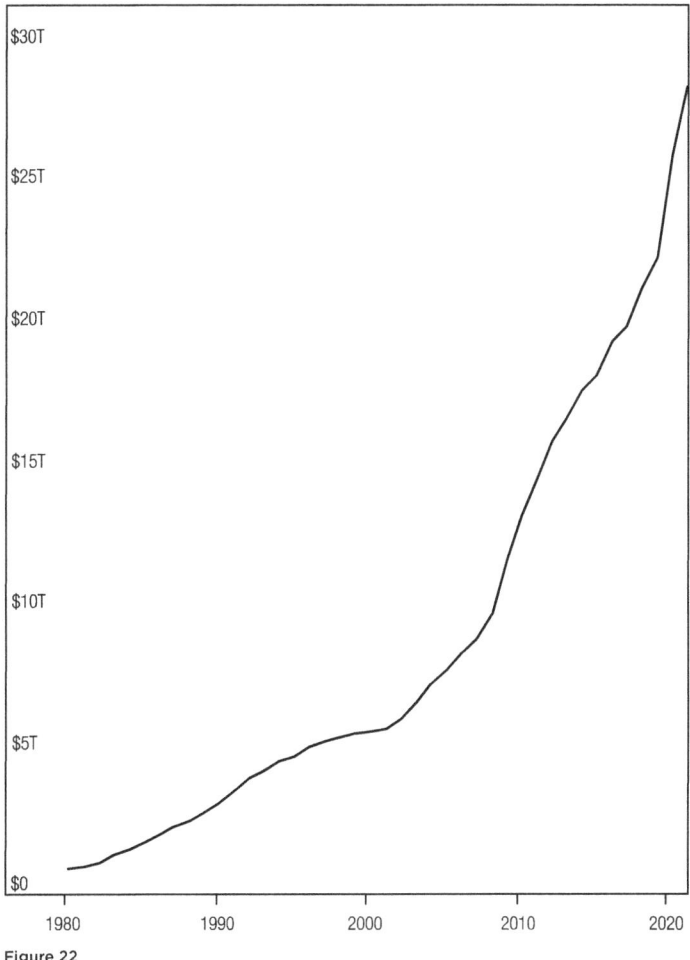

Figure 22

When Bitcoin's price rises, other altcoin prices rise in US dollars, but their price against Bitcoin is what should matter most to an investor. It's important to consider the BTC pairing for an altcoin to determine if it's a better investment than simply holding Bitcoin. There are brief rallies in altcoins that can create upward moves against Bitcoin, but they are typically short lived and more challenging in terms of time of entry and when to exit. There are some experienced traders who may be successful at this, but for many people, it can be a losing battle.

I've tried to be a trader in the past and it sometimes feels insane staring at charts and taking in technical analysis from other sources all day, only to lose money on trades and deal with the mental anguish of feeling manipulated by an irrational market. Emotional swings and anxiety can become a problem. I've seen posts on Twitter from addicted crypto traders who go broke, beg for donations, and in the worst case are offered suicide hotlines to avoid ending their own lives. Being responsible with money requires checking the internal greed meter once in a while and refraining from attempts to get rich quickly at the risk of losing money needed for necessities. For me, this has led to less speculation over altcoins and a more consistent approach of holding the asset that continues to reign supreme: Bitcoin.

SELF-CUSTODY

There is one lesson I learned early on that I've always followed, and that is to own the private-public key pairs for the assets I own. If the keys are not mine, then I don't own the crypto. It's as simple as that, but the temptations are out there to either send crypto to a service for yield or custody assets for convenience. Keeping a balance on an exchange can easily lead to losing access to assets. Even if the service to custody assets has secure vaults with titanium-etched keys and an army of guards, it's still not my asset if I don't have the keys. The digital assets space is still early in its development, and many companies that manage assets will seem trustworthy on the surface, but how can they be trusted? A fancy website and marketing materials mean nothing. There are countless stories of millions and billions of dollars' worth of digital assets being lost, stolen, hacked, and frozen, leaving the rightful owner with no recourse. Although this may seem like an overplayed broken record rant, it is surprising how many people, both new and experienced, get bitten by breaking this simple rule. For one thing, Bitcoin's ethos is fundamentally based on decentralization and self-reliance. It's a practice just as much as it is a technology. In my experience, it's enlightening to learn how to self-custody and manage assets.

There is a feeling of empowerment and earned experience associated with being responsible for moving more than a million dollars with a transaction. It motivates the user to really understand the mechanisms that are at play and become more responsible in the process. I don't think it's a great idea to send a million bucks' worth of crypto on the first go since mistakes can be made. Remember, I first started out with $1,000 worth of Bitcoin in total and made a simple purchase to test things out. Even if someone doesn't want to invest, it can be rewarding to try to play with the technology to see how it works.

I've often found that I can explain how it works, but if I'm talking to someone who has never used it, the explanations are often ineffective. There are many articles, videos, and courses online that can help newcomers get started. All the necessary tools to try using Bitcoin are free, and test networks exist for the purpose of executing trial runs for new features or updates to the core software. These testnets can be used to experiment with cryptocurrency assets that don't have market value but can be used to execute features in the core wallet software. Even though I am not qualified to offer any investment advice, I certainly advise everyone to learn more about custody and wallet technologies to better secure their assets.

INFLATION

Proponents of Bitcoin and other scarce assets have long held the belief that a fixed supply asset will act as an inflation hedge, meaning that scarce assets preserve their purchasing power in an inflationary environment. In late 2021 when the CPI rose to levels not experienced since the 1980s, this caused some confusion among the investment community when Bitcoin's price started to go down quickly after the CPI went up. Many commentators were quick to point out that Bitcoin must not be an inflation hedge if this price inflation coincided with a drop in digital asset values against the US dollar. The problem with this claim is one of language semantics: the conflation of CPI and the concept of monetary inflation. CPI is a year-over-year percent increase in consumer prices, using a weighted calculation based on a basket of chosen product categories, such as shelter, energy, and food. This means that even if prices are consistently increasing every year, the inflation rate year over year remains constant. In fact, our Keynesian central planners believe it is a good thing to maintain a rate of inflation around 2 percent because it motivates spending instead of saving, and this is by design to promote a higher velocity of money in the economy. On the other hand, monetary inflation is when the money supply grows, and this doesn't always make the prices of products go up because much of this capital can find its way to other investments, such as funding a new business or buying stocks and digital assets. New money invested in R&D might even lead to lower product costs if the research leads to cost-cutting innovations.

The government can more easily justify borrowing money when interest rates are low, and sometimes that results in handing out stimulus checks or government programs designed to ease financial pressure on consumers. The coronavirus pandemic resulted in a massive wave of this type of new capital in the economy, and at the same time, lockdowns caused people to close businesses and stop key operations in global supply chains. People received stimulus checks to offset the downward pressure on economic metrics, such as GDP growth and stock portfolios. The initial result was a massive upward move in stocks and other assets, but months later in 2021, the supply shortages started to create an imbalance in supply-demand dynamics, causing prices to skyrocket.

Even before Russia invaded Ukraine in February 2022, inflation was at levels not seen since the 1980s, and gas prices had already almost doubled from the previous year's low. When Russia finally did invade Ukraine, Western governments applied sanctions on Russia's central bank, and Western companies began exiting the Russian economy, which only increased the upward pressure on price movement in oil, and gas prices skyrocketed. In July 2022, the CPI rose to 9.1 percent, a forty-one-year high not seen since 1981.

It was in November 2021 when the Fed first mentioned a policy reversal to combat rising inflation. Instead of continuing to increase the assets on their balance sheet and keeping near-zero interest rates, they would begin decreasing assets on their balance sheet and raising interest rates. This announcement in November was a reversal from the inflationary monetary policy to deflationary tightening, which explains the sudden exodus of capital in assets such as Bitcoin in the weeks that followed. So, even though CPI remained high and went higher for the next six months after the November 2021 Fed meeting, the markets were responding in a deflationary way to the planned monetary tightening policy. They anticipated that the economy would slow down, and some companies would go bankrupt and/or lay off employees. This is why Bitcoin and equities markets are "forward looking," as they attempt to price in future policy changes and their eventual effects, which can take months or even years. The timing of these moves led some to believe that Bitcoin's price was not an inflation hedge, but this is a very short-term reactionary view given that Bitcoin was still far outpacing price inflation given a long enough dataset. For example, investing in Bitcoin two years prior to the day of the 9.1 percent CPI print would have returned over 100 percent on the original investment, even after the early 2022 Bitcoin wipeout to $20,000. At the high of $69,000, Bitcoin's return over those years was closer to 700 percent in less than two years. Going back further in time only increases this rate of return, suggesting that variables other than CPI have more influence on Bitcoin's price, such as adoption rates and monetary expansion causing excess liquidity to be absorbed into assets. The heightened CPI in 2022 led to the deflationary policy reaction from the Fed, and monetary tightening gave the markets enough reason to rotate out of risk and into various safer havens to preserve wealth.

THE FIAT INSURANCE POLICY

Somehow, I always find a new way to think about Bitcoin. After years of watching Bitcoin do pretty much the same thing fundamentally from a technology perspective, it would seem to make more sense that nothing new or interesting should emerge out of its continual and relentlessly consistent presence. However, in the complex world of money, there are so many interrelated dynamics that the subject never becomes dull. As more experts in the field of finance find themselves sliding into Bitcoin's event horizon, new research and perspectives appear more and more interesting as time goes on, and the educational value of the community almost seems to outweigh the monetary value of the network.

One recent perspective that came across my feed was the application of Bitcoin as an insurance policy against the historically likely decline of the world reserve fiat system. The way this has played out for centuries, in various empires, would appear to be baked into our genetic code based on how inevitable it appears to be, and similar processes have taken place in isolated cultures outside of Western empires. The way a long-term debt cycle typically plays out, it will eventually lead to a decision with a binary choice. One outcome is that the government must practice austerity measures and increase taxes to pay for its previous expenses, both of which are politically unfavorable. The other option is to create more debt to continue to finance the previous expenses.

Austerity measures and taxes are politically detrimental for the leaders in power, and a self-reinforcing feedback loop develops where the more debt buildup there is, the more debt is needed to continue satisfying popular demands. This can be exemplified on a small scale in a single-family household. If the family doesn't have the money for a bigger house as the family grows, it's not typical that the one in charge of the finances breaks the bad news that the family will now have no vacations, be downgraded in education costs, and eat ramen for dinner every evening just so that the family can save the funds needed to afford a bigger home. Nor do the parents take their kids out of school and put them to work, collecting their paychecks, effectively converting the family into a makeshift sweatshop. Instead, it is more popular to take out a home loan to finance the new home, making a promise of generating more money from future income to be able to pay off the interest over time. In a similar way, the government takes out more debt to service its previous debts and continues to pay for new government programs to appease its citizens, ensuring a positive outlook to gain support and avoid civil unrest. Even though this printing of new debt creates the effect of debasing the currency, people still see the same number of dollars in their bank account, so nothing appears to be lost at first, but decreasing the purchasing power of existing dollars is sometimes described as a hidden tax on the public at large.

Bitcoin is an asset that counterbalances this debasement mechanism like the way an insurance policy is a countermeasure to an unexpected financially disruptive event. Because of this inverse relationship that an asset with a fixed supply maintains, Bitcoin is effectively an insurance policy for monetary debasement. Given the populist phase that the United States has experienced in its political environment and skyrocketing government debt since 2008, the dollar-based premium on this insurance (the USD/BTC price) has been rising sharply for the past thirteen years. If the debt cycle plays out like it has historically in every other fiat currency-issuing country ever to exist, owning some insurance may be prudent.

CHAPTER 9

THE FUTURE

MINING AND ENERGY

A popular point of contention between Bitcoiners and **no coiners** is the debate regarding climate change and energy consumption. Bitcoin mining uses electricity, and the statistics typically used to denigrate miners compare the network's electricity usage to small countries or isolate the statistics so they aren't compared to equivalents in terms of delivered value. This isn't to say that Bitcoin mining does not have an impact on climate change or the energy grid, but a wider perspective is necessary to understand how Bitcoin mining compares to other consumers of electricity to weigh the benefits against the costs.

According to a study by Cambridge University, Bitcoin mining was estimated to consume 121 terawatt-hours of power per year. But an even more recent paper called "Bitcoin Cryptopayments Energy Efficiency," published in 2022, provided deeper insights and uncovered some significant deviations from previous studies. The total power consumption in the new study came in at about half the original Cambridge estimate at 88.95 terawatt-hours per year. Even though this number sounds large, for comparison the study goes on to show that the traditional banking system is estimated to use around 4,981 terawatt-hours per year, or about fifty-six times as much as the Bitcoin network. Another factor is the incentive to use cheap energy to maximize profits in the mining sector. This cheap energy incentive has resulted in a high ratio of renewable and/or sustainable energy usage for mining and has also drawn miners to unexpected places to find innovative ways of using waste energy that would not have been used at all.

A company called Vespene Energy is using methane emitted by landfills to generate energy for Bitcoin mining. One of the key reasons mining is a good use case for waste energy is that mining rigs are very portable. One of the expensive aspects of energy production is transmission over long distances and distribution infrastructure, but if miners capture the methane energy at the source to monetize the otherwise unused wattage, then it becomes a viable method to reduce greenhouse gas emissions in places where the energy would otherwise be hard to transmit over long distances.

Another use case for mining that is taking hold on some energy grids is the capture of runoff electricity where power production infrastructure is built to produce a minimum capacity with intermittent sources such as wind and solar. To fund a green energy project can be challenging when intermittency requires base load backups and a minimum production capacity for times when wind and sunshine are deviating to their lows. Because of this, on days when there is plenty of wind and sunshine, there is extra runoff energy that can't be used/stored easily or cheaply and doesn't get absorbed by consumers, so it is often wasted. Bitcoin mining to the rescue!

Yet another property of Bitcoin miners that fits perfectly into this equation is the ease at which the hash rate and energy consumption can quickly be dialed up or down on demand to maximize runoff monetization and can also react quickly to shortages on the grid. Other runoff solutions exist, but they often present challenges to dynamically ramp up or contract consumption quickly and reliably, limiting the ability to maximize the economic viability of these renewable energy installations. In the future, I expect to see many new innovations in the energy space, and Bitcoin mining will almost certainly play a role in the ongoing progression toward more sustainable energy production.

RETAIL VS. INSTITUTIONS

Bitcoin was the first digital asset to prove that scarcity could reliably be implemented in a decentralized internet-based system, and early in its existence, most adopters were technology enthusiasts. The droves of traders and technical analysts that trade in the space now did not exist in 2009, and the market was lacking the tools to allow serious capital to enter the arena. In 2017 during Cycle 3, there was some early adoption by institutions, and some hedge funds began to implement strategies for digital asset holdings. The first US commodities futures instrument was launched by the CME on December 17, 2017, right before the crash leading into the bear market in early 2018. Since then, an avalanche of institutional players have entered the cryptocurrency space as discussed in the history of Cycle 4. The term "retail investor" refers to a nonprofessional who can make trades on their own through an online broker or exchange. Up until 2017, the cryptocurrency markets were dominated by retail participants, but after 2017 leading into Cycle

4, it became apparent that the pros had entered the game with their strategists and algorithms. One reason this is important is that a lot of charts and history may no longer be as useful in today's crypto investing environment given the evolution in the market over the last five years.

Considering that cryptocurrency trades twenty-four hours a day and seven days a week, it is already a different beast compared to traditional markets, but there are still rapid changes in motion as the asset class matures. One difference I've noticed is that the weekends used to be when retail investors had spare time to trade, so often, volatility would occur on Saturdays, Sundays, or holidays. Now this has reversed to an extent in my observations. I've seen weekends become calmer, and stock market open hours have coincided with volatility in the digital assets markets. Sometimes non-US market hours also determine price action to a degree. As the market gains new participants, these factors change and evolve, so there is no telling how different things will be if adoption continues the S-curve to a billion users. What is clear is that when big institutional capital has skin in the game, it will change the market dynamics in the future, and my theory is that it will make retail trading much more difficult. Going up against pros in the trading game is not likely to get any easier over time as more and more institutions have piled in, so I've become more interested in bigger-picture macroeconomics that can filter out the short-term noise and help with defining a strategy for the long term.

USABILITY

Technology tends to trend toward being more usable over time. Initial iterations of new technological tools can be cumbersome to utilize and, in many cases, initially require expert-level knowledge in a field such as engineering to defeat the usability barriers that prevent the masses from adopting new tools. Eventually, a technology that has the potential to be widely adopted becomes more usable over time as entrepreneurs recognize the value proposition of a particular product or service and invest the capital to make advances in developing more usable iterations. For example, the internet is a tool that initially required specific knowledge and access to effectively participate in the network. Early iterations of the internet were not only much smaller networks with strict access, but any user would have had to have technical industry knowledge regarding the protocols that were developed to send data using the underdeveloped technology. Early versions of the World Wide Web didn't have well-calibrated search engines. I remember in the early '90s, the typical method of accessing a website was to type in specific URLs and save frequently accessed sites in bookmarks. I created some of my first web pages using HTML to aggregate links so related sites in various categories would be easier to access, and these sites racked up thousands of hits in a time before millions of users were engaged with the online world.

Today, browser address bars act as both a search field and an address entry field, so it's often the case that the web is accessed via search rather than typing in specific URLs. I still use bookmarks, but it's surprising how often I'll simply type in the name of a company or service, initiating a search, when I could simply add the ".com" at the end of the name in most cases to get to the site directly. Search has become a habit, and it makes navigating the internet much easier.

Payment system technology is an area where usability advancement can increase adoption of Bitcoin. Although an act as simple as giving money to a merchant in exchange for a good or service might seem trivial, that is largely because many companies develop systems that hide the complexity of transactions and generate a significant revenue stream for their products and services.

According to the 2021 McKinsey Global Payments Report, $1.9 trillion in payment revenues were recorded for 2020. There are many popular companies competing over this revenue generator such as Block (formerly Square), Stripe, Braintree, PayPal, Venmo, and many others, but it would be a shame to forget that the early pioneers in electronic payments were the credit card companies, such as Visa, Mastercard, and American Express. In the early days of credit cards, there was a particular chicken-and-egg problem that arises often in technology adoption cycles where not enough users hinders motivation to offer the product or service, and therefore support for the product or service is seldom offered. Such was the case with credit cards initially because not many people had them, so merchants weren't motivated enough to accept the cards, suppressing adoption from a user perspective. This barrier was eventually defeated when in 1958, Bank of America launched BankAmericard in Fresno, California due to the city's high concentration of banking customers. Bank of America delivered 60,000 cards to customers in the same city and convinced merchants based on this penetration to accept the card at their establishments.

In the early days of credit card use, the technology was primitive and required an imprinter, which is a device that the merchant would place the card into with layers of carbon paper, such that sliding a bar over the paper would imprint card information on an invoice. This manual process didn't check for stolen cards or maxed-out balances, so merchants would must either cross-check the card number against a book of reported stolen card numbers or deal with potential disputes when credit card issuers refused to settle charges.

It wasn't until payment terminals accepting credit cards could validate a transaction with a remote service that the merchant could be better protected from disputes over charges. Visa led the move to electronic PoS systems in 1979, and new players followed, such as Verifone and Ingenico with initial products launching in the early 1980s.

Payment systems have evolved to support many features including merchant services that provide automatic accounting capabilities that integrate with many business management software suites. This allows companies that accept payments to take in high volumes of payments from many locations and centrally monitor activity in near real time. At the 2022 Bitcoin conference in Miami, Florida, Strike announced integration with Shopify and NCR, adding Bitcoin payment processing to PoS systems. These systems are designed to make the conversion from BTC to fiat pairs automatic so merchants can choose to avoid absorbing volatility in the Bitcoin price and accept payments in the currencies of choice or even dial in exact percentages of a sale that will be paid in Bitcoin versus local currency. The goal is to mask all the complexity involved in working with Bitcoin addresses and converting currency pairs manually, while directly interfacing with the payment processor to seamlessly transact from a customer point of view, and provide the merchant with the tools needed to accept digital asset payments without requiring domain knowledge to manage a new form of money.

In the future, I expect that more merchants will be accepting Bitcoin without even having to work for it due to these seamless integrations provided by Strike, NCR, Blackhawk, Shopify, and others that integrate with Strike or other Bitcoin payment systems. This could eventually lead mobile payment providers like Apple Pay or Google Pay to compete or partner with solution providers such as Strike to activate Bitcoin payments on terminals that accept mobile payments.

Anyone who has experience manually dealing with Bitcoin transactions would easily understand the need for integrated systems to remove the technical complexity from the user's point of view—that is, if Bitcoin is going to have any success as a form of money used to transact in a marketplace where ease-of-use competition is present. Existing solutions tend to trade off security and/or privacy for usability. Security may never be ideal in the case of reliable, fast, and easy payments, and scalability (based on transaction bandwidth) may always trade off with decentralization, but it is ultimately up to the user how much they can tolerate in terms of handing off responsibility to a trusted party.

One of the fascinating aspects of Bitcoin is the awareness it brings to the masses regarding things that would otherwise go unseen or are in plain sight but easily taken for granted. I never thought I'd put so much time into understanding how money works until I discovered Bitcoin and became determined to understand the reasoning behind decentralization and its value to what has become a fast-growing base of users. But if those users all must first have college-level engineering degrees to operate the network manually, I fear that most potential users will be sitting on the other side of a chasm without the technical ability or the patience to use the technology, just as many potential users of the internet sat on the sidelines until computers became user friendly enough to provide easy access. Bitcoin is inspiring engineers, designers, and payment providers to step up to the challenge of delivering solutions that empower people to have control over their money, while also making it easy and seamless to use it.

DISRUPTING THE STATUS QUO

In the late 1400s during the medieval period in Europe, printing was in its early phases of being able to scale up the information pipeline across the continent. The result of lowering the cost and time to produce printed reading material led to the adoption of literacy, which took on the form of the familiar S-curve pattern.

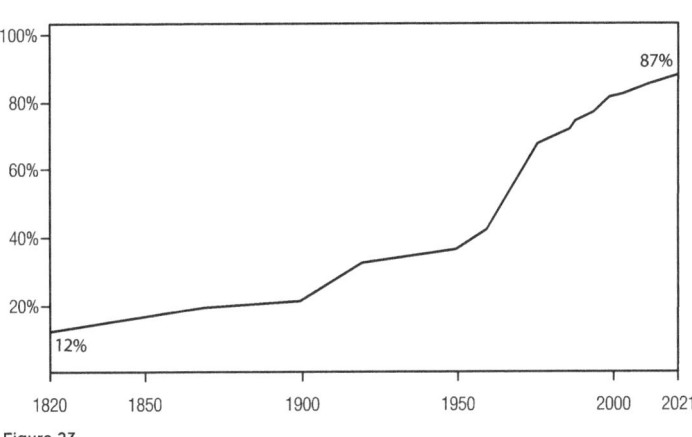

Figure 23

The new ability to quickly absorb different perspectives through reading reminds me of the internet's ability to connect people and enable its users to communicate at the speed of light, allowing many cultures to share ideas, argue, and pontificate over everything people often do. The printing press enabled widespread literacy and gave people multiple perspectives that would have previously been inaccessible, opening a whole new conscious range of human thought at scale.

New and diverse ideas led to a fracturing of opinions like an epistemological explosion culminating in the Reformation and the Thirty Years' War in the seventeenth century. The value systems eventually coalesced again into more refined ideas that inspired the age of Enlightenment. Today, a similar pattern of fragmenting values is emerging with the information superhighway online. Each account feeds data back into the source of information such that algorithms and often artificial intelligence determine the next bit of information to present to the user.

Social media going mainstream is highly correlated with some alarming trends in politics and social behaviors, especially in younger generations that have no life experience in a world without the internet. A fracturing of values and new ideological trends are taking shape as the binding forces of Enlightenment values are dismantled and give way to postmodern philosophy challenging universal truths. The forces of evolution are at it again with the introduction of conflict to challenge the status quo, inspiring us to navigate a new set of values and possibly even new religions as was the case with the Reformation. The new printing press is upon us, and internet literacy has also taken the S-curve path to mainstream levels of adoption.

It is my intent to contribute constructively to the process of rebuilding the value systems and worldviews that will give humanity the tools it needs to continue to survive. I can't be 100 percent positive that Bitcoin is going to be a major component of our existence down the line, but its appearance and influence on our world starting in 2009 is significant to the history of human ingenuity, and with each block and each new user contributing to the adoption curve, the global human consciousness is breaking through a barrier that may lead to an evolved mode of existence in the future, given that there is a new way of thinking about ledger technology and how rules in the system can be enforced. All monetary systems will now be competing in a world that has decentralized ledger technology. The internet was utilized to replace bookstores, newspapers, record shops, and snail mail and is now finding a way to incorporate the concepts of money and ownership in a system native to the network itself.

Regardless of whether the result is widespread usage of one of the original blockchain projects, such as Bitcoin, or some other yet-to-be-determined system, it is apparent that the existing traditional system is being challenged and will continue to face stronger challenges as technologies evolve to compete with the status quo.

CHAPTER 10

THE BIG PIVOT

In June 2022, as I continued to do research on markets and put the final touches on this book, it occurred to me that something historic was taking shape about the global economy, the US dollar, and the Federal Reserve. The United States appeared to be entering an economic transition and had no plans to end the Ukraine-Russia conflict abroad but instead seemed to be instigating further war and disruption in the world order. By applying sanctions on Russia as a reaction to the invasion of Ukraine, the United States set a precedent that the dollar can be used as a weapon at the whims of the powers in the West, and other world leaders took notice of this move. Rumors of a new reserve currency being in the works hit headlines, and it was the Brazil, Russia, India, China, and South Africa (BRICS) alliance that was dabbling with the idea of conducting international trade with an alternative to the dollar. When I saw this announcement and saw the Fed jawboning about inflation and how they felt the need to tighten monetary policy to slow demand, I picked up on a new potential motivation for keeping the rate hike regime on regardless of collateral damage. This appeared to be an escalation in a currency war, and the dollar was the defending champion.

China began more lockdowns in major cities, citing COVID-19 as the reason, but it came off to me as a suspicious set of moves at a time when reduction of manufacturing output was suspected to be a significant contributor to inflation in Western nations, including the United States, which had printed a consumer price index at over 9 percent. For some (still mostly unknown) reason, Nancy Pelosi, the Speaker of the House at the time, took a trip with a military convoy to Taiwan without clearance from the Chinese Communist Party (CCP), which warned the United States as Chairman Xi Jinping stated in a call with President Joe Biden, "Those who play with fire get burned." It was after Pelosi's trip that the CCP ramped up military exercises around Taiwan, even sending missiles directly over the island.

My wife happened to be traveling through Taiwan to get home from Malaysia at the time, and we were lucky that all China Airlines flights were still on time bound for SFO, dodging the missiles on their way, I suppose. Then there were also announcements of cutbacks in manufacturing deals with US companies. Some of this unraveling may have already been set in motion with the CHIPS and Science Act, passed on August 9, 2022, which ramps up regulations on semiconductor manufacturing abroad. However, the Pelosi trip to Taiwan accelerated the conflict, and it's likely that more developments are to follow that could erode US-China relations even further.

Chinese leadership has stated that they reserve the right to reintegrate Taiwan into China and will do so by force if necessary. The Pelosi visit appeared to solidify the United States' support of Taiwan's independence, and President Biden has claimed publicly that the United States would defend Taiwan if attacked by China's military forces. There does not seem to be a clear path for US and Chinese leadership to both get what each is saying they want, and a peaceful resolution only seems further from reach now as relations between our nations continue to crumble.

THE DOLLAR MILKSHAKE

In 2022, as the Fed tightened monetary policy by raising interest rates faster than at any time in history, other foreign central banks could not keep up and their currencies started declining quickly against the dollar. Other countries have large amounts of debt denominated in dollars and use dollars for global trade. When dollars get more expensive to obtain, it means a country that desires to service its debt will pay more in its own currency for new dollars to service previous debts with new debt, and the cycle repeats. This process adds recursive demand pressure for dollars, which can lead to some relentless self-reinforcing processes, and continue to drive the dollar higher in value against other currencies. For example, a country might decide to sell US Treasuries on its books to obtain more dollars instead of taking out new debt in local currency to buy more dollars. This dumping of Treasuries causes bond yields to rise on top of the added dollar demand it causes, hence the higher servicing cost of debt in dollars worldwide, leading to yet more dollar demand to service debts around the world.

The United States is in effect fighting inflation at home by exporting inflation to other countries that have less stable currencies and bond markets. This phenomenon of increasing dollar demand has become known as the **dollar milkshake theory**. In this scenario, the US dollar will appreciate against other currencies and cause US imports to be more affordable while making exports sold in exchange for dollars harder to afford for foreign customers of goods and services produced by the United States. In other words, the dollar being more relatively valuable in the world economy helps to resolve inflation problems at home in the United States while ratcheting up the problem in other countries. This also adds downward pressure on the price of oil against the dollar, which leads to lower gas prices and a higher approval rating for the sitting political administration. Aside from oil, other commodities generally reprice inversely to the dollar, and this helps to fight inflationary pressures.

Unfortunately, while a stronger dollar may sound like a good thing for Americans, it comes with difficulties for pretty much everyone, including Americans who own assets in an overly financialized economy. The dollar is a counterweight to the stock market and assets priced in dollars. When the dollar is appreciating in value, stocks and other assets are typically falling. Although asset prices coming down is good for new investors who are waiting for an opportune entry point, it does not guarantee consumer price inflation is getting better in all categories. By strengthening the dollar, other countries' inflation rates are going up faster than they are in the United States. This is also not good for the US economy, which relies heavily on product sales in Europe, China, Japan, and many other countries that are now facing currency volatility, sovereign debt risk, and the heightened possibility of a recession. If the Fed creates enough demand destruction, causing a recession while inflation is still hot, the economy endures a **stagflation** phase, which may be the worst possible outcome for the US economy.

PEAK INFLATION?

As the Fed increased funding rates in the early months of 2022, the US stock market started to become volatile and endured some sizable losses. After a deep decline ending in June, the S&P 500 was down about 24 percent from its highs and the NASDAQ was even worse off at around a 34 percent decline. What caught my attention was that many accounts on social media seemed to believe the bottom was in and began reinvesting, although I was skeptical.

The Fed had stated that the plan was to continue to raise rates to fight inflation, which was still coming in at a forty-year high of over 9 percent. A month later in July, CPI came in at 8.5 percent, and this was the first indication that inflation may have peaked, and that is when the next major rally kicked off in markets. I used this rally as an opportunity to liquidate my remaining assets to preserve cash, and by mid-August, it was apparent that liquidity was starting to dry up in the economy. The Fed was nearing the date at which they would start reducing their balance sheet, which had grown to be over $8.9 trillion, mostly consisting of bonds and mortgage-backed securities. The balance sheet is suspiciously tied to the stock market moves seen in recent years, and the last time QT was used in 2018, it came with a crypto crash and drawdowns in the stock market as well.

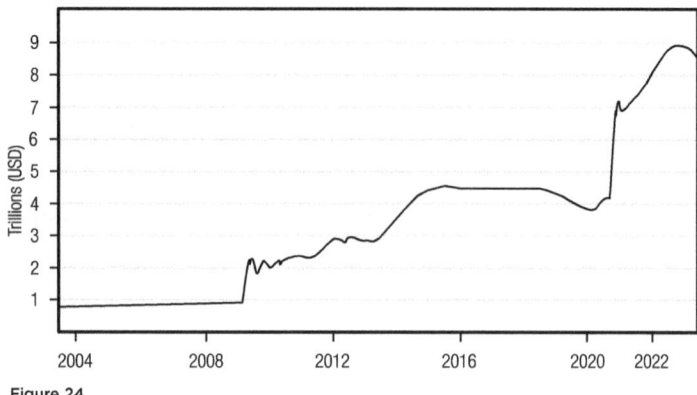

Figure 24

With QT, which began in August 2022, and a planned continuation of interest rate hikes, it made me look back to times of inflation over 8 percent in the past. What I realized is that the stock market doesn't do well in these periods, and the dollar tends to rise during times of high inflation. Bitcoin especially has not done well when the dollar is rising, but even more interesting to consider is the fact that Bitcoin had only existed during times of QE and expansion of the Fed's balance sheet (with a short exception in 2018) while inflation remained quite low, starting with the genesis block in 2009 right after the 2008 bust, and enjoyed the extended asset bull market that continued on without seeing a traditional widespread bear market. This meant that it could be the first time Bitcoin and all cryptocurrencies were finally preparing to experience a global bear market and possibly even a new depression cycle like the one that started in 1929 just after the Roaring Twenties bubble ballooned with the help of loose Fed policies. I imagine not many people are prepared to manage risk in such an environment because I and so many others alive today weren't around to experience the market tragedies of the 1930s. Even worse is the fact that our conditioning in markets is based so heavily on central bank intervention, including bailouts and government handouts in populist fashion. This conditioning is Pavlovian and can cause people to expect bailouts anytime there is any sign of a decline in the economy. What if those bailouts caused hyperinflation? Would that cause the United States to follow the path of Weimar Germany in the 1920s, out of which the rise of the Nazi Party was infamously a derivative outcome?

Aside from the fear of populism fomenting the rise of extremism in politics, it is also discomforting to live in a society that loses its ability to recognize self-sufficiency and responsibility to produce value at the individual level. This effect on the population causes irrational behavior in markets and bizarre "good is bad, and bad is good" contrarian logic to take hold. When up is down, left is right, good is bad, and a recession is seen as good for stocks because the Fed will step in and pump up markets with fresh new liquidity, the ability to invest for good reasons such as backing legitimate companies goes out the window and a period of incessant speculation emerges. The trend is clear when considering the growth of the financial sector and its absorption of talent, including engineers, scientists, physicists, mathematicians, statisticians, and many people who would otherwise be producing innovative solutions to societal problems but find themselves grinding on the goal of turning money into more money in the world of finance.

PEAK IRRATIONALITY

In August 2022, even though I was doing research and finding that the situation we were in was likely leading right into the next big recession, social media was abuzz over the "inflation has peaked" narrative, but there was also the concept of a "Fed pivot" gaining popularity in social media circles. The concept of being in favor of a Fed pivot posits that the Fed will stop raising interest rates and stop QT because there is too much pain in the markets and the economy for the Fed to continue fighting inflation. Cheering on a Fed pivot suggests that people only care about numbers in their portfolio going up and have complete disregard for the real economy and what it means to allow rampant inflation to intensify. A proponent of a Fed pivot would seemingly prefer hyperinflation to resetting the economy to some form of rational baseline where price stability is achieved. I realized that the market had been conditioned in a way that was completely unhealthy. Even some of the most experienced investors I had followed on social media began betting on a pivot, which didn't play out through 2022, and Fed chairman Jerome Powell killed those expectations in December 2022, indicating that there would be no such pivot until inflation was clearly on its way to 2 percent. Inflation remained at over 7 percent through the end of 2022, nowhere close to the Fed's target.

I had witnessed the progression of politics becoming more populist during the period between 2008 and 2022, and it all started to make more sense as I connected the dots between monetary policy and historical political disputes throughout history. The building up of an asset bubble is exactly the type of progression that leads to irrational markets and extremism in politics due to increased wealth gaps and economic instability, but it happens so gradually over time that it's difficult to realize it without the awareness of what to look for. It took looking back through data and charts on all the previous years, wondering why Bitcoin's price seemed to go up around the time of election cycles, and looking at many other asset price charts to realize that all assets had been a sponge for the excess liquidity created over the years by central banks. That excess was originally justified to solve a political issue or save the economy from imminent collapse, but now it was just fiat value propping up assets that quite obviously did not have the ability to produce the expected future returns given the now-higher interest rates and rate of inflation, which would prove to be stickier than many people expected in the following months.

In a time when inflation could legitimately spiral out of control, many people were cheering it on so their portfolios could go up as priced in dollars. The ironic thing is that by betting on a pivot and keeping excess money allocated to speculative assets, the bet on a pivot eases financial conditions and provides a tailwind to inflationary pressures. This dynamic of persistent inflation causes the Fed to continue to tighten monetary policy even further to counteract the excessive inflationary forces in the economy at large. In other words, betting on the pivot makes the pivot less likely.

The Fed seems to work in a vacuum and only has the responsibility to maintain a couple of key metrics. One of these is price stability (inflation) and the other is unemployment. This is what the Fed calls its **dual mandate.** If unemployment remains low, or under about 4.5 percent, then it is the Fed's mandate to also ensure inflation remains low at a target of about 2 percent. If jobs are still plentiful, which they have been in 2022, this means the Fed is unlikely to pivot to lowering interest rates, and all the pivot speculators could end up getting wiped out by a continuation of tightening policy, which provides strong enough headwinds to destroy the bubbly wealth created by loose policy over the last fourteen years.

If we do get a pivot and go back to QE and zero-interest rate policy, then the US economy would be at risk of entering a period of heightened inflation and asset bubbles causing even wider wealth gaps, increasing the potential for civil unrest and an unhealthy political environment. With the recent statements coming from the Fed stating that they will not pivot without seeing inflation definitively on the way to 2 percent, it gives me hope that I've witnessed peak irrationality, and even though the economy may go through a recession, I for one would be ecstatic to see many of the inefficiencies and overfunded **zombie companies** die off so that more resources can be dedicated to the truly productive and valuable endeavors in our economy.

THE FIRST MACRO BEAR MARKET FOR BITCOIN

If Bitcoin goes through a global recessionary period for the first time, it could cause a drastic decline in unit price and market capitalization. As liquidity is drained from the system, people might eventually need to sell Bitcoin and other assets to pay for essentials if inflation eats away at the ability to afford the same lifestyle, and if the dollar continues to strengthen, then assets will continue to be repriced lower against the dollar. Many people are holding on through the volatility, but I imagine if inflation takes another year or more to come down, as history suggests is probable based on prior battles with high inflation, many asset classes will depreciate in dollar-denominated terms as the economy digests higher interest rates for an extended duration and a reduced central bank balance sheet over time. The outcome could be very similar to the dot-com bust in 2001 where projects that survive may come out on the other side with more strength and proven resilience in the long term. It's in periods like these that an asset such as Bitcoin could thrive as an alternative to traditional assets. Perhaps this will not come in the form of mania over pumping prices but rather an objective analysis revealing the benefits of having sound money that is managed outside of the traditional system. Uncertainty looms over the global economic order as we know it, and leaders appear to be losing control by the looks of market volatility and the increasingly drastic measures taken by central banks around the world.

An important metric to track through this potentially tumultuous period is user adoption because the more uncertain our situation tends to be, the more precious metals and other scarce assets become attractive as hedges against uncertainty. As the younger and more technologically savvy generations take over for the pre-digital-age leaders, there may continue to be growing support for technically superior ledgers and money with the added benefit of being decentralized. Bitcoin's rise in popularity represents progress toward a realization that the control and power over money in central banks and governments is overbearing on the world as central policymakers flounder again and again, trying to steer the ship, both too late and too much, before realizing that their decisions are too many degrees of separation away from the forces that naturally create balance in the economy. Bitcoin is a decentralized alternative to the centralized fiat regime, and as long as the fiat money system continues to be unstable, Bitcoin gains adoption and thrives. Perhaps policymakers will take notice of the trends and make changes in the existing system to support a more stable and efficient centralized monetary system. Ultimately, it is the market that will decide what it values most in the end.

GLOSSARY

Alt season—A term used in the cryptocurrency world to refer to a period when alternative cryptocurrencies, or altcoins, experience a surge in price and market capitalization relative to Bitcoin. During an alt season, many altcoins may see significant gains in value, with some even outperforming Bitcoin.

Altcoin—A term used to refer to any cryptocurrency that is not Bitcoin. The term "altcoin" is short for "alternative coin" and was coined to describe the many new cryptocurrencies that emerged after Bitcoin's initial release in 2009.

BASIC—Stands for Beginners' All-purpose Symbolic Instruction Code. A high-level computer language created at Dartmouth College in 1964.

BitTorrent—A decentralized protocol that allows people on a network to share and copy files, such as movies and music.

Black swan event—A term used to describe an unpredictable, rare, and extreme event that has significant and far-reaching consequences. The term was popularized by Nassim Nicholas Taleb in his 2007 book *The Black Swan: The Impact of the Highly Improbable*.

Blockchain—A linked data structure that contains all transaction history in a cryptocurrency network and facilitates a decentralized consensus mechanism providing trustless validation abilities.

Blockchain trilemma—The blockchain trilemma proposes a set of three main issues—decentralization, security, and scalability—that developers encounter when building blockchains, forcing them to ultimately sacrifice one aspect as a trade-off to accommodate the other two.

Bretton Woods Agreement—An agreement in 1944 between the United States, Canada, Western Europe, Australia, and Japan to guarantee currency convertibility to within 1 percent of fixed parity rates, with the dollar convertible to gold at $35 per troy ounce of fine gold. This agreement made the US dollar the world reserve currency, allowing foreign countries to settle transactions with a common asset that is easier to divide and transfer than gold.

Buy the rumor, sell the news—A phenomenon where an upcoming event causes market participants to buy an asset in anticipation of the event being positive for the asset valuation. The anticipation of the event is what causes price to appreciate, and the event taking place is when profit taking occurs.

Capitalism—An economic system where capital can be invested with the goal of generating future gains.

Cold storage—A method of storing data or digital assets offline in a secure and isolated environment. This is done to protect the data or assets from potential online security threats such as hacking or cyberattacks.

Consumer Price Index (CPI)—A year-over-year percent increase in consumer prices, using a weighted calculation based on a basket of chosen product categories such as energy and food.

Cryptocurrency—A cryptographically secured digital asset transferred via the internet.

Dollar milkshake theory—A theory popularized by Brent Johnson that attempts to explain how demand for US dollars can increase in a time when other countries rely so heavily on obtaining dollars to pay off debts and pay for imports such as oil.

Dual mandate—A term used to describe the two objectives that are assigned to the United States Federal Reserve by Congress: to promote maximum employment and stable prices.

Everything Bubble—A scenario brought on by stimulative financial conditions where central bank policies support appreciating asset prices with the expansion of monetary supply and low interest rates. The Everything Bubble often refers to a time of financialization in the US economy that started with the introduction of quantitative easing in 2008 and continued until 2022 as many assets reached all-time-high valuations.

Exchange—A marketplace, typically accessed on a website or mobile application that allows users to deposit funds and swap various forms of currency and/or assets at an exchange rate set by the market.

Fiat money—Money that is declared to have value by decree, typically issued by a government that accepts tax payments in a specific currency.

Flippening—A term used to refer to a hypothetical event in the cryptocurrency world where the market capitalization of Ethereum surpasses that of Bitcoin, making Ethereum the largest cryptocurrency by market capitalization.

Fractional-reserve banking—Fractional-reserve banking is a banking system in which banks are required to hold only a fraction of their deposits as reserves. This allows banks to create new money through lending, as they can lend out more money than they hold in reserves.

Full node—An instance of software services that maintain a full copy of the ledger/blockchain for a digital asset such as Bitcoin.

Gas (Ethereum)—A term used in the Ethereum network to refer to the unit of measure for the computational effort required to execute a transaction or smart contract on the network. Gas fees are paid when users transact on the Ethereum network. Simple transactions cost less in gas than more computationally complex transactions.

Genesis block—The very first block in the Bitcoin blockchain, mined by Satoshi Nakamoto on January 3, 2009.

Google Cardboard—A virtual reality (VR) platform that uses a simple cardboard viewer and a smartphone to create an immersive VR experience. The platform was first introduced by Google in 2014 at its annual developer conference, Google I/O.

Howey test—A method of determining whether an asset should be defined as a security. Passing the test suggests that the asset is in fact a security and not a commodity or in any other asset class.

Initial public offering (IPO)—An event where a company's stock is first offered on the public stock market.

Liberalism—A philosophy that emerged in the late Renaissance inspired by rationality and objectivity. Liberalism would later become the dominant philosophy that inspired the United States Constitution and the prevailing world order today.

Logarithmic regression—A logarithmic curve fit to data to describe the relationship between adoption and historical value of Bitcoin and other assets or technologies.

Macroeconomic environment—The macroeconomic environment refers to the overall economic conditions of a country or region, including factors such as economic growth, inflation, employment, and monetary policy. It is a broad assessment of the economic health and performance of an economy.

Market cycle—An arbitrarily defined demarcation of macro market swings from lows to highs and back to new lows. A cycle typically includes a bull market phase where price climbs to a new top, followed by a bear phase where price declines to a low before starting a new cycle.

Memes—A term originating from the short form of memetics, originally described by Richard Dawkins in *The Selfish Gene* published in 1976. A meme is typically used in social media environments to quickly spread ideas, often using clever images and/or phrases to get a point across.

Mempool—A list of unserviced transactions waiting for miners to process. A growing mempool typically means that more transactions are being attempted than can be serviced, potentially creating delays for users and higher transaction fees. Transactions that offer higher fees are prioritized by miners.

Modernity—The historical period between the seventeenth century AD and the late twentieth century AD, characterized by the rise of the Industrial Revolution and rapid scientific progress. The exact time is often disputed.

Moore's law—Based on a prediction by Gordon Moore, the law states that the number of transistors that fit in a fixed area of space increases exponentially over time.

Mt. Gox—Stands for Magic: The Gathering Online Exchange. One of the first Bitcoin exchange websites where fiat money could be deposited and traded for Bitcoin.

No coiner—A person who does not own any Bitcoin or other cryptocurrency assets.

Ponzi scheme—A scam where new investors create the profits for early investors and/or creators of the scheme, typically promising high rates of return using fraudulent data to lure in new participants.

Pre-mine—An early token issuance typically distributed among creators and early investors of a new cryptocurrency before allowing other investors and miners to create new tokens.

Private-public key pairs—In asymmetrical encryption, a public key can verify ownership of a private key without exposing the private key to another party. A public key is used as an address like a unique email address that allows Bitcoin participants to send a portion of their unspent balance to the owner of a public-private key pair. A Bitcoin owner must use the private key to sign transactions to send BTC to another public address.

Proof of stake—Proof of stake is a consensus mechanism used in blockchain networks to validate transactions and create new blocks. A proof of stake validation node proves ownership of a staked asset and validates transactions in return for compensation. Unlike mining in proof-of-work (PoW) systems, the proof of stake validation process does not require solving complex math problems. The pros and cons of PoW and proof of stake are debated regularly in terms of power usage, security, decentralization, and scalability, among other concepts pertaining to effective consensus in digital ledger technology.

Pumpamentals—Pumpamentals is a term that combines the words "pump" and "fundamentals" and is often used in the context of cryptocurrency trading. Pumpamentals can refer to reasons an asset will pump in valuation without necessarily having underlying fundamental value—for example, a marketing campaign with a celebrity.

Security—A fungible asset that is traded in a market under a regulatory framework, typically with the intent to profit from the investment and typically relies on a third party to generate gains. For example, shares of stock in a company are securities regulated by the Securities and Exchange Commission.

Sound money principles—A set of economic principles that emphasize the importance of stable and reliable monetary systems. Sound money systems are characterized by limited supply, stable value, transparency, decentralization, free markets, and security.

Stablecoin—A type of cryptocurrency that is designed to maintain a stable value relative to a specific asset or basket of assets, such as a fiat currency like the US dollar, gold, or other cryptocurrencies.

Stagflation—A state in the economy in which consumer prices are inflated above a desired threshold and the economy enters a recession with high unemployment and stagnating economic growth.

Stimmy check—A colloquial term used to refer to the stimulus checks that were distributed by the US government in response to the economic impact of the COVID-19 pandemic. The stimulus checks were part of the Coronavirus Aid, Relief, and Economic Security (CARES) Act, which was signed into law in March 2020.

Stock-to-flow ratio—A ratio of the stock or supply of an asset versus the rate of production or increase in supply over a specified time interval. The formula is a simple tool that can measure relative scarcity of an asset. A higher stock-to-flow ratio indicates a higher difficulty to produce more stock added to the total supply. An asset with fixed supply would technically have infinite stock-to-flow since the flow in the denominator is zero.

TCP/IP—Stands for Transmission Control Protocol/Internet Protocol. A standard for implementing reliable data communications between networked devices.

Triffin's paradox—Triffin's paradox was developed by economist Robert Triffin in the 1960s and is often cited in discussions of international finance and monetary policy. The theory explains the tension between a country's domestic economic goals and its global reserve currency status as it relates to the world reserve currency issuer.

Unit bias—The tendency to favor unit price as a measure of value rather than evaluation of total market capitalization.

Wallet—A digital wallet is a software application that can manage the public-private key pairs that represent ownership of a cryptocurrency asset.

White paper—A document that describes the purpose and functional details of a cryptocurrency asset.

World order—A widely agreed-on system of rules and regulations that guide world trade and economic activity between countries.

Zombie company—An unprofitable company that continues to operate if it can take out debt or receive bailout capital to cover expenses.

Milton Keynes UK
Ingram Content Group UK Ltd.
UKHW010656030324
438663UK00011B/157/J